NO ROAD MAPS

NO ROAD MAPS

By Margaret P. Allen

Founded 1910
THE CHRISTOPHER PUBLISHING HOUSE
HANOVER, MASSACHUSETTS 02339

To C.B.
And for Our Families
Past, Present and Future

Table of Contents

Chapter 1

The Golden Wedding

I was nine months old, when church bells and train whistles announced the arrival of the twentieth century. But I actually entered it ten years later, when our family made the hundred-mile journey to my grandparents' golden wedding anniversary celebration in an automobile.

In 1910 automobiles were toys for rich sportsmen, not transportation for middle class families. Yet here we were, an ordinary, slightly upper-middle class family of five, about to charge together into the twentieth century — in a touring car — at 10 to 15 miles an hour!

A golden wedding anniversary (when life expectancy was less than fifty years) was also a rare event. Grandma Harris, who loved company, must have planned months for this — to have her three sons, one daughter and nine grandchildren all together at one time under the high roof of the verandahed Victorian house which she and Grandpa Harris had shared for years with family, friends and impoverished students in the pretty college town of Amherst, Massachusetts.

This was long before the then State Agricultural College had become the great University of Massachusetts. In 1910 Amherst was *The College*, a small, beautiful bastion of academic excellence.

The four families would be expected to arrive by train — from the Boston area, from New Jersey, and from faraway western New York State. Grandpa Harris no longer kept a horse, so he would arrange for them all to be met by the local livery stable team at the little Boston & Maine railroad station.

Our father had other plans.

As the one son-in-law, he undoubtedly saw an opportunity to make an impression of elegance and affluence on his wife's family. Actually, he always delighted in what was new, different, adventurous, and of the future.

He told our mother he was going to hire one of the new touring cars (with a chauffeur, of course) and the Pratt family would travel to Amherst and the Golden Wedding by automobile.

I can imagine her reaction.

"Will! Isn't that *dangerous?* Won't it *cost* too much?"

Today, that trip from Wellesley, up the Massachusetts Turnpike, and off at Palmer, where the low Pelham hills beckon, takes about two hours. In 1910 it took us TWO DAYS.

The 1910 touring-car in which the Pratt family made the 100-mile, two-day trip from Wellesley Hills to Amherst, Mass. The photo was taken by the chauffeur at our roadside picnic stop the first day. Father has taken his place at the wheel. Note right-hand drive and suitcases tied to the running board.

Mother had us all out of bed and dressed in the fresh July dawn. The night before, she had made stacks of sandwiches, stuffed hard-boiled eggs, cut cake squares, folding all in linen dish towels, wrapped in a linen tablecloth, and packed in our family picnic basket.

We had never heard of "soft drinks," and Mother disapproved of iced tea for children. So she had hand-squeezed a dozen lemons, chipped ice from the fifty-pound block in the back pantry icebox, and filled mason jars with sweet lemonade. Oh, yes! There was also a lemon meringue pie. Our little brother, Harris, was to get sick on it, and never, in a long life, touch lemon meringue pie again.

Because of that delay somewhere en route, or perhaps as a result of so many flat tires (which Father and the young chauffeur wrestled off, patched, pumped up with a hand pump, and pounded back on again under the hot July sun), or more likely because even the chauffeur didn't always know which dirt road to turn down, the end of that long, hot day found us only as far as Springfield. I remember a hot hotel room, and Mother fanning us children, her starched white shirtwaist and long, black linen skirt hanging limply over a straight chair. Hotels then had few closets, no hangers.

The touring car was open on all sides and had no windshield. Father had bought his three "girls" long, lightweight linen coats, called "dusters." We tied big, pale chiffon veils over our straw hats, to keep them from blowing off, and also to layer in front of our noses.

Father and Harris (strong males!) had only linen caps, pulled down over their ears, to protect these and their eyes from the clouds of yellow dust, from flies, bees and mosquitoes, and from the sharp scent of horse manure, all of which swirled 'round our heads. The chauffeur had a black derby, with which he fanned himself — when he wasn't hanging onto the wheel with both hands.

It was an exhausting (it must have been an expensive) excursion; but worth it all (at least to Father) when, in the late afternoon of the second day, we drove proudly — *loudly* — Father pumping the rubber-handled horn — up along Grandpa Harris's vine-covered porch.

The "verandahed Victorian" of my grandparents, Prof. and Mrs. Elijah P. Harris, Woodside Ave., Amherst, Mass. as it appeared in their lifetime. Prof. Harris in front.

Tall uncles, fashionable aunts, curly-haired cousins, Grandma Harris — plump and perspiring in her silk "afternoon dress" — Grandpa Harris — stout and startled out of his academic musings — and, in the background as always, Mary Sullivan, wiping her floury hands on her long, white apron — all crowded out the door, squealing, screaming, exclaiming in excitement and wonder at the Pratt family's dramatic arrival in Amherst in an *automobile!*

The Harris and Pratt family group at the Golden Wedding anniversary celebration July, 1910 in Amherst. Wearing pigtails, I am standing directly behind my grandfather, Prof. Elijah P. Harris, with sister Betty and brother Harris to my left. Back of Harris is Grandma's "Help," Mary Sullivan, and my parents are standing to her left.

Today, more than eighty years later, I can still see stout little Mary Sullivan, with her pockmarked face, and her thin gray hair twisted into a bun on the top of her head. Her like no longer lives.

She was an orphaned Irish immigrant, who had somehow become a member of the Harris household. She did not know where or when she had been born (a tragedy to three children whose birthdays were always celebrated). No one, apparently, knew or cared whether she remembered her Irish home, a Catholic faith, or the green and misty land of her birth. Her cooking was her Calling; her Cloister — the

Harris home; her Service — the Harris family. When they were gone, Mother and Father found her a comfortable room, and nursing care at the end. For almost seventy years she has lain buried in the midst of all those Episcopalians and Presbyterians, in the quiet family lot under the oak trees that look off to the Pelham hills.

We probably made the trip home by train — I do not remember. Trains were the way one traveled in the early 1900s. And oh! the excitement and grandeur of travel by Pullman! Dinner in the dining car; the friendly black faces of waiters who liked children; the multitudinous silverplate; choosing from a menu, instead of being told to "Eat what's on your plate!" (but discreetly check the prices and don't choose the most expensive dessert); savoring each mouthful, while the strange countryside rolled by. People waving at crossings — waving at *us*! The delicious feeling of speed and danger, as one crossed from one swaying car to another over the racketing wheels, the air suddenly fresh in one's face.

All this delight was followed by going to bed in a lower berth. You tucked your unmentionables into a string hammock, instead of draping them over a chair. There was the strange sense of being part of the great world, yet safely isolated from it, as you snuggled down on soft pillows, switched off the light, and lifted the shade just enough to see the dim lights of lonely farms slip by, while crossing-lights and bells flashed, jangled and vanished, as the train bored on into the darkness of a distant destination, not to be discovered till morning.

Our mother kept her best lace and lawn nightgown for her occasional overnight train trips.

"If there's a wreck, I do not intend to be picked up dead along the tracks in one of those old flannel things you babies threw up all over!" she explained.

But we returned from Amherst to the familiar routines of walking to school, to church, to the stores. It never occurred to any of us (except possibly Father) that our family would ever own an automobile.

Today's two- and three-car families cannot begin to understand what life was like before the century of the motorcar. We drive to work, to school, to shop, to see sights and visit friends two blocks — or a continent — away. We drive to get something, to get away from something. We are always going some place — any place —

no particular place. And nobody, in 1910, could have imagined our jammed highways, blocked beltways, our big city gridlocks, our exhausting waits in endless lines that jerk forward — stop — start — STOP — while the air thickens with fumes and frustration.

Nor, in 1993, can anyone recall a land without four-lane, six-lane, *eight-lane* highways; a land without drive-*ways*, drive-*ins*, drive-*ups*, drive-*throughs*. There are only a few of us left to remember the green, the quiet — and the dust!

To be sure, when we were children, we had our Sunday drives. Behind a rented horse, in a surrey — yes! "with the fringe on the top." Father held the reins, Mother sat beside him, the picnic basket at her feet. The three of us children squirmed and squabbled on the back seat, demanding a picnic spot with a brook, so that we could take off our black-buttoned shoes and long black stockings and wade in the cool, running water, where there were no rusty beer cans nor rotting tires to block its gentle flow.

In the early years, Father had had his own surrey, and a matched team of horses, "Nellie and Dan." I was afraid of them, as I was afraid of all animals, but Harris adored them. His first spoken word was "horse." At seventeen he was a member of the National Guard cavalry outfit stationed in Boston, which was called out for duty during the Boston police strike that propelled Calvin Coolidge into the vice-presidency.

Perhaps I was especially afraid of horses because sister Betty and I came near being killed by them.

We were on our way, hand in hand, to kindergarten, Mother watching our block's journey from our front door, when a runaway team of horses swung 'round the curve and bore down upon us. I remember hearing shouts, and turning to see the great, frantic beasts, with their high, huge, pounding hooves, slashing the short stretch behind us. We cowered helplessly back against the yard fence, as the driver sawed on the reins. At the last second, the horses swerved, missing us by a couple of yards. And we turned — sobbing, stumbling — back toward home, still clutching hands.

A few years after the Golden Wedding, Father returned home one day driving a new Kissel car. It was OURS! We accompanied him in awe and ecstasy around the block, while he explained the mechanics of driving. Seventeen miles an hour, he explained, was the proper driving speed — safe but not stodgy.

The "Blue Books" came with the Kissel car days. Their rich, dark blue covers were stamped in gold, and they told you just how to get from a number of *Heres* to an equal number of *Theres*, distances usually twenty to perhaps fifty miles.

"Proceed ½ mile to fork in road, with white church on left. Go four miles with fence to river bridge. Bear right after crossing bridge 1½ miles to..." And so on.

Mother held the Blue Book on her lap, reading the directions to Father. And it says much for their marriage that there were few arguments, and we usually got where we were going.

I don't remember when the Blue Books gave way to road maps, which used to be given away every time you bought gas. But three generations of Americans have grown up on wheels, expecting — as a matter of course — to get where they're going. Signs blossom on rural roadsides, or shout from giant super-structures along the Interstates. At 65 miles an hour, who could look at a book?

Sometimes, though, one finds oneself on a strange road, a long way from home, with few, if any, signs and it is beginning to get dark...

Where is the road map for the *Nineties*? Not the 1990s — the age nineties?

The *Sixties* are following the thruways to Florida. The *Seventies* write books about coping with old age — when they are not sifting through retirement home brochures, full of photos of smiling white heads above raised glasses.

The *Eighties* are *in* the retirement homes, but they are not smiling as in the slick folders... So many silent, gray-haired women, sitting alone in the comfortable lounges, waiting... For what? For whom? And white-haired men — my brother was once one of them — pacing restlessly. Nobody needs them now. Nobody wants them.

And the *Nineties*?

We hear America's population is aging. We visit former friends in nursing homes,and are appalled at the fraility, the futility, the senility in long corridors and in silent rooms, where only the TV chatters.

How well I remember — God forgive me! — my own young impatience with those who stumbled and fumbled and mumbled. Now *my* feet falter and my fingers fail to function. When few reached sixty, old age was a wonder and a reverence. Now it is a problem, and we are a nuisance.

Individually, we may be respected or admired, but often we are considered downright difficult. We want someone to tell us what to do, but we push away the helping hand at the elbow. We seek the special consideration due old age, but resent no longer being one of the crowd.

While I've always regretted the children that never came, there's a certain satisfaction in not having anyone who feels it necessary to arrange your present or plan your future; in making up your own mind, and not feeling guilty because the children would feel less anxious, if you were safely stashed away somewhere.

"Pretty expensive, yes! But Mother will be well cared for and we won't have to worry over whether she's eating right or might have a fall. And she'll be with nice people her own age."

My own age! Ninety-three. How dreadful!

That's why I always end up pitching out the beautiful retirement home brochures. I want to be around people who are *doing* something — planting gardens, painting pictures, pounding the typewriter, putting their kids or themselves through college. I don't want to talk about my aches and pains or the latest sit-com. I want to talk to painters and politicians and teachers and little Girl Scouts who come selling those dreadfully dry cookies, and to small boys who want to shovel my driveway to get money for... what do small boys buy nowadays?

Years ago a long-time friend (we had both been widowed) said — "You and I are lucky. We don't *have* to do anything any more."

I thought about that for quite a while. I guess I had always assumed I had to keep on getting up, getting going, getting things done, getting to bed, getting up... If I didn't *have* to — should I?

Then I realized she had quit traveling, had sold her car, stopped going out, was no longer seeing friends. She hired a housekeeper, because she didn't feel like doing housework; later, a secretary, because she didn't feel like answering letters or balancing her checkbook; then — because she was spending so much time in bed — nurses 'round the clock. Pretty soon she no longer could get *out* of bed.

We had long talked and laughed and gone places together. Now I could only inquire as to her condition. Even before she died, I had lost a friend. But even before her death, she had left me a legacy: the knowledge that it's more fun to try to do things, to keep pushing, than to say "I don't feel like it."

Obviously, I've been on the road a long time. The sun is low on the horizon, and I'm vague about the distance ahead . . . I wish there was someone to *ask*!

Most men don't want to stop and ask directions. They'd rather keep going and hope they've made the right guess. But I always like to stop and ask questions.

Of course you don't always get the right answers. Sometimes you'll be told "Sorry. I don't know."

Sometimes you'll be misdirected and have to backtrack.

But sometimes you'll find those who know the way.

I remember Miss Annie.

Chapter 2

Dad and Miss Annie

No woman wants to shut the door on her loved possessions and go live with a daughter-in-law — and a stepdaughter-in-law at that! Nor does a wife look forward to sharing her home with her husband's parents. I know *I* did not. But, then, C.B. was home safe and sound after three years of overseas duty in World War II, and I was not going to complain about *anything*.

Dad and Miss Annie were both over eighty, and the time had come when they could no longer live alone on the isolated Kansas farm, which had been Miss Annie's home since childhood, and where C.B.'s dad had settled in with her, after they married, both for the second time.

The cows were long gone, the pasture rented, the garden grown up in weeds; only the chickens were left to sell. So Miss Annie packed their clothes, her rug pieces, Dad's chewing tobacco, and the snapshots of her great-granddaughter, and turned her face eastward, with gentle dignity and no complaints.

C.B. and I were living in a little old New Jersey house on the edge of suburbia, which we had bought and restored in the late thirties. From here he had been recalled to active duty in the Air Corps, and to here — thank God! — he had returned. But, with the war over, we were planning a journey down a road well-known to twentieth century Americans: the young shake the country dust from their feet and head joyfully for the city; in middle age, they buy a farm and return, delightedly, to the country.

In our case, the farm was C.B.'s childhood home in West Virginia — a high house of weathered pink brick, with a low log-and-frame wing; empty for years, neglected and withdrawn in a tangle of brush along the stream bank. It was to be home for over twenty years, and in sharing it for the first three with Dad and Miss Annie, I was to learn much about traveling strange roads with hope and faith.

11

Dad had never liked Kansas, though he'd stood it fifteen years on Miss Annie's account, and felt it had not been in vain, when the state turned up in the 1932 election in the Democratic column. But he didn't approve, he said, of folks who drank wet and voted dry.

Not that he, himself, drank much, as he had told a doctor who examined him when he was in his mid-seventies.

"Now then, Mr. Allen, do you ever use any intoxicating liquors?" the doctor had inquired.

Dad would have pressed his fingertips together, as he always did, when considering his words.

"I have catarrh in the mornings and, to clear my throat, I some-times gargle a little gin," he told the young man in the white coat. "I am not always able to spit it all out."

Dad was in Kansas when the state first went dry, and he told us how the saloon owners, unable to sell their stock, invited friends in to help dispose of it. Once, as they sat drinking, a man raised his glass and cried, "I give you a toast! Nectar for the gods!"

The next night an old German said, "Poys! I gif te toast!"

Raising his glass in clumsy imitation of the other's debonair gesture, he cried, "Poys! Necktie for Cheesus Krise!"

But now that Dad was well into his eighties, and if he were about to die — "and it's the last thing I'm a-goin' to do!" — he wanted it to be back home in West Virginia. And if he were going to live awhile longer — as began to seem likely, once he no longer had to cope with the Kansas well and the pile of soft coal in the yard — he hungered to talk over old times with old friends, see the sun go down behind the hills, where it belonged, have a snort of Wilbur's corn, and vote once again in the Democratic primary.

Just once in his life he had almost voted Republican.

"I bin sorry, some, since," he admitted. "He wa'nt on'y a Repub-lican, he was a former major in the Union Army. I fergit his name now, but when he was in the State Senate, he sponsored a bill to re-enfranchise Southerners. He was a good man, too, and the man who ran against him — Annie, do you recall his name? — he wa'nt worth a damn. But I couldn't bring myself to vote Republican."

At eighty-seven, the tales that had evoked laughter or caused astonishment lingered in his mind, but the words to make them live again no longer came readily to his tongue, and he would turn and ask — "Annie, just what was it that feller said?"

No matter how deep she was in a magazine or book, Miss Annie always had the right answer. That was the only way we knew she had heard these tales time and time again. But even when she sat beside him, quietly busy with her sewing, she was not re-living memories. She knew that down that pleasant road, old age lies waiting. The young, they say, live in the future, the old in the past, but the wise live in the present. With no advantages, with little education, Miss Annie was a very wise woman.

We learned to anticipate her effect on friends and acquaintances. When such arrived, Miss Annie was just an elderly relative, to be treated courteously, but with no great attention. But there was nothing perfunctory about their good-byes. And she never failed to remember that it was Billy who was writing the novel, Bridget who was pregnant, and Betty who helped set out the strawberry plants.

Somebody once asked her if she were happy, having left behind her home, her relatives and the wide Kansas horizons, to live with her husband's family, a thousand miles east in the shadow of the hills.

"I carry my happiness with me," was Miss Annie's gentle rejoinder.

They may well have wanted to ask how she and her stepdaughter-in-law managed to work harmoniously in the same kitchen. It was all Miss Annie's doing. She never proffered advice, never insisted on doing things *her* way. She watched, and did her best to master another's routine. Coming, however, from a land that knew desperate droughts, it was hard for her to run enough water in the dishpan.

Miss Annie's formal religion, I suspect, stemmed from grim Calvinist roots. I say "suspect," for we never had any religious arguments. There would have been no point. Her practice of it was pure, shining Christianity, and there was nothing to argue about there. Anybody could see she made it work.

I demurred once, when she wanted to kill a blacksnake.

"C.B. says they're good for the garden. He says they eat bugs and mice."

"Maybe so," Miss Annie retorted, "but they also eat little chickens, and the Bible says thou shalt bruise his head and he will bruise thy heel. Now, hand me that hoe and I'll bruise his head good and plenty!"

Her life had been spent wringing a hard living from a hard land, a life totally isolated from the world of news headlines. So now she gloried in having a New York newspaper to read.

From the radio (television was yet to conquer the mountains) she would have no soap operas. I guessed there had been too many real tragedies in her own life for her to enjoy make-believe ones. If there wasn't news, she wanted music. But Dad didn't fancy sopranos.

"Kill her! Kill her!" he'd command.

So Miss Annie would put down her sewing and start twisting the dial.

"Wherever my father went, he'd start a singing school," she commented once, when music made her rarely reminiscent.

"In Pennsylvania where he first worked in the mines, and later when we homesteaded in Kansas. My! he had a good voice! Everyone of us sang or played."

"Did you ever take music lessons?"

"Yes. I started once but I had to stop."

"Why?"

"Seemed as if I couldn't think of anything but the music, once I set down to the piano. Dinner or chores — I'd forget them all. So I had to stop. The work had to be done."

When television did reach Hardy County, West Virginia, the first set belonged to an old man living alone up on top of Branch Mountain. He had it installed in his bedroom, because, back then, only late night shows could be received. He would turn it on, and when he awoke at one or two in the morning, his bedroom would be full of folks from the hills and hollows, who had come quietly in (there being no locks, of course, on his doors) to hunker down silently and view the wonder of the black and white screen; and who would as quietly leave, when the show was over.

The years Miss Annie lived with us, we never heard her say anything about her son's father, though Dad had once said, darkly, that he was a railroad man who drank. We wondered about her first marriage. Did she feel it unseemly to talk about it, now that she was Dad's second wife? Or was it that her first marriage had been an unhappy one?

We knew only that, when her first husband died, she went to her father, who was old and alone, and made a deal to buy the Kansas farm and care for him the rest of his life. Days she worked in the fields, returning at dark to her housework. Her son struggled beside her to the limit of his boyish strength, one back breaking year after another, ending in crop failure and more debt; until finally, the young man gave up and went to Kansas City and a haber-dashery job. But Miss Annie stayed on the land and, eventually, the debts were paid and the farm prospered modestly.

Dad and Miss Annie at The Willows, about 1947. He has his hickory stick in hand.

At eighty-three, her feet — which had never known better than the cheapest mail-order shoes — "bothered" her a lot, though that never kept her from going with us when we went to walk in the hills. So did her "weak stomach," nourished too often, she said, on "cold bread and strong coffee," which had stood half a day on the back of the stove. So did her back, which had strained for years to handle hay bales and corn shocks.

"Stay in bed and let me bring you breakfast," I urged more than once.

But even as I spoke, Miss Annie's small, twisted feet would be feeling for her bedroom slippers, while she smiled at me over her glasses.

"At my age, you better not start giving in to yourself, or you'll find you're not good for much," she would say.

At *my* age, I keep trying to remember that.

You cannot, these days, pick up a magazine or turn on the TV without being told how to stay young and desirable. Miss Annie's hair was gray and sparse, her figure short and dumpy, her hands knotted with rheumatism. But her back was straight, there was a sparkle in her eye and a laugh in the corner of her mouth, and when a waltz would lilt over the air, her foot would tap discreetly. You could understand why a man carried her memory for forty years in some small corner of his heart, so that, when he had buried his first love, he would go back to find his second.

She was a dressmaker's homesick little apprentice in a Kansas frontier town in the 1880s. The warm spring wind was blowing straight from her home on the prairie, and in the darkness, she put her head on her arms on the windowsill, and cried.

Across the street, a young man, come from the East to make a stake so he could go back to West Virginia and marry his girl, called out softly:

"What you cryin' about, Annie?"

"Nothin'," she answered, wiping her eyes.

"Nothin' ain't nothin' to cry about then," he told her. "But if you're homesick, you git up at four tomorrow morning. It's my day off, and I'll get a team from the livery stable, and we can be down at your mother's for breakfast. But don't be late! The horses won't stand."

She wasn't. And they drove across the unfenced prairie, with the dawn breaking behind them, and her mother gave them a good farm breakfast.

That's all there was to it, except maybe a dance or two, and the good-bye kiss she wouldn't give him — she said she didn't like his moustache! But it was enough, after forty years, to take him back to Kansas. And if Miss Annie was homesick in New Jersey or West Virginia, no one ever knew it.

The first year they were with us, she saved seeds from my New Jersey flower beds to plant in her Kansas dooryard when she returned home. But in the West Virginia spring, I found her scattering the contents of a large envelope in a bare bed down along the yard fence.

"You said you'd have to buy some seeds for here," she answered my question.

"But aren't those the ones you were saving to take home?"

"Yes, but you need some flowers here, and we jest as well be enjoyin' 'em this summer, while we can."

No sighs for the slow realization that it would be a long time before she could return to Kansas; and perhaps never again her own garden to work herself. No clutching to herself of the mantle of martyrdom which many women enjoy wearing; no worrying over an uncertain future. Just the cheerful acceptance of the present as the time to live and love and grow a garden.

I had to go hunt up a hankie.

"I ain't afraid to die!" Dad had declared more than once. "Why should I be? I never cheated nobody, and all my life I set up with the sick. There ain't a family in the Valley where I ain't set up with somebody who was sick or dyin'. Set up all night and go to work the next day... But I was younger then."

He must have been a good nurse, too, for there was a gentleness in him in spite of his quick temper. He was nurse and housekeeper for all the years "Miss Sallie" lay bedridden. So it seemed fitting that his second wife should give him the same devoted care he had given his first.

Death is headlined every day, in the papers or on the tube, but we do not accept it as part of life. We can deal with funerals, because they have become spectacles, and we are used to such. But we are afraid of death. It forces us to face the beliefs we have ignored, the faiths we have forgotten.

World War I produced the saying — "There are no atheists in fox-holes." Standing at the bedside of someone who is dying, one is acutely aware that all around, life is moving on. This quiet moment is like time spent in a waiting room at a railroad station. It is necessary before the journey along another line will eventually begin.

"Alice! Come get me!" Dad would plead from the depths of morphine-induced unconsciousness, to his best-loved sister, who had died fifty years before. Listening, we could not but feel that Alice was waiting there somewhere across the edge of eternity, where he could, perhaps, just glimpse her.

We put a flower in his buttonhole and his stick in his hand. The hickory stick had been cut forty years before, and the top had the satiny feel of antique furniture, while the tip was a ferrule made from an old shotgun shell. He never went anywhere without it.

Once, when he flew east from Kansas to visit us, work schedules made it necessary to have him met. Telling about it later, he said:

"I ain't never laid eyes on this young feller before, an' I got to thinkin' how the devil he walked right up an' called me by name. So I ast him.

" 'Oh,' he said, 'Your son, Carl, told me to look for an old man with a hickory stick in his hand.' "

Twice now, in her lifetime, Miss Annie had stood at the graveside of a man she had loved and lived with. Each in his own way had loved her, but they must have been very different ways. She would have known that Dad would never drink too much, nor easily spend money; that he would work hard and look for laughter along the way. But the only time he gave her a present was when he brought her flowers after he had hunted her up in Kansas forty years after their last good-bye. He was right pleased with himself for having thought of flowers. He told us about it any number of times. But it never would have occurred to him to buy them for her after they were married.

The day after the funeral, Miss Annie sat at the breakfast table, her face drawn with the strain of grief and sleepless nights — she was never one for the easy oblivion of sleeping pills — and told us the little we were ever to learn about the man she had first married. It was as if this second loss had raised the flood level of her memories to where words must spill over the dam of her reticence, built high through long, lonely years.

"I had the nicest clothes! Matt loved to see me dressed up. And hats! I always had the newest, prettiest hats in Kansas! Matt was dining car steward then, and he used to like to have me ride on his train. Of course I had a pass! Nothing was too good for me in those days. He bought me a diamond ring, too.

"It's all gone now. I wasn't no different in those days from any other young, heedless thing. It's easy come, easy go. You think the good times will last forever, and then one day you have to take hold and buckle down."

She had done it. With love and loyalty. And without bitterness.

We resorted to every argument of love and need to keep her with us. But Dad had told her that, after he died, he wanted her to "go back to Kansas and look after Molly." We were a little appalled when we learned that Miss Annie proposed to do just that: take her eighty-five-year-old cousin with a broken hip back to the farm, and look after her and the place both.

"I can raise a few chickens, enough to pay for our groceries, and Molly'll be happier with me than in town," she explained.

"But Annie darling, the farm has been untended for five years, you don't know what shape the house is in! And anyway, it wouldn't be safe for the two of you out there by yourselves. Suppose you got down. What would happen, with Molly not able to walk?"

It was a long time before Miss Annie was willing to admit the impracticality of her proposal. She didn't really admit it, she just finally said, "Well, once't I could've done it," and agreed to go to a sister-in-law's in town.

Five years she had waited to go home, and now it was not to be. Anyone who has felt the pull of home and long-loved possessions can understand what must have been her heartache, as she packed her homemade dresses, her feed-sack aprons, her rug pieces, and the snapshots of her great-granddaughter. If there were tears, we never saw them. If she was worrying about her future . . . But Miss Annie had always known better.

"Sometimes we get the habit of wondering about what the next day will bring forth," she said, "instead of living the day we have to our heart's content."

So Miss Annie refused to let her uncertain future spoil her enjoyment of the October glory without, and the comforts of automatic heat within. That future was to offer a bleak Kansas winter among relatives on whom her five years' absence had wrought the inevitable changes of illness and age; followed by her grandson's small, crowded home in California.

So, at eighty-nine, she found herself a job — looking after an old lady of eighty-five, who "didn't have all her buttons" and would turn on the gas stove without remembering to light it. In her nineties, her legs and feet gave out, and she had to go to a nursing home. There, in her wheelchair, she spent her days visiting the bedridden, the depressed, the difficult, forgotten or ignored by their own families, until — after her hundredth birthday — she died quietly in her sleep.

A dozen years before, we had put her on the plane at National Airport, a short, sturdy figure in her navy blue suit ("I went out and bought it — brand-new! — to stand up in and be married to your Dad. It cost *twenty-five* dollars!") and a new black hat ("Do you think the feather looks foolish?").

We must each fight back the salt pressure of tears, as the motors roared and the plane turned down the runway, lifted off and headed west.

"Good-bye, Miss Annie! Good-bye! And God go with you."

As if He hadn't! Always.

Chapter 3

Our Family

It was because of what I learned from my own parents that I could cherish C.B.'s.

When my father entered a room, people always looked up. It was not just that he was a tall, good-looking man; he projected optimism, anticipation, enjoyment; kids and dogs always sidled over to be touched and talked to.

Talk! Whatever interested anyone instantly intrigued him; he was eager to give and receive information and opinions. His probing, restless mind constantly sought insights, solutions, simplifications. For him, the future always promised fulfillment — for himself and for mankind. He was always certain it must bring him more time and money to spend on his family.

Yes, he was naive; gullible, even. But he believed passionately in the goodness of God and man, and in the glories of the coming age. A marvelous man to take a child to a museum or a circus or a library!

Fifty years after his death, I can still see his hands, so charged with energy; their short, spatulate fingers drew, carved, mended, soothed. Surgeon's hands they might have been.

He had, indeed, wanted to be a doctor, but suffered some sort of breakdown in his youth which greatly limited the use of his eyes. The doctors of his day prescribed a sea voyage. So he sailed around the world on a square-rigger. And we three children grew up on his sea stories, learning ships' rigging, absorbing weather lore, and listening to Kipling's poetry, which he loved to read and recite.

When we buried him (following a brief heart attack at age 68) in the Amherst cemetery which looks toward the low hills, we had the simple stone engraved with lines from Kipling's *The Palace*, which seemed to him to sum up his own life:

All I had wrought I abandoned to the faith of the faithless years.
Only I cut on the marble, only I carved on the stone:
"After me, cometh a Builder. Tell him I, too, have known!"

Mother grew up in Amherst, only daughter of a beloved college professor, adored by three brothers, in a home always full of the presence and talk of young men — their exploits, their dreams. Her brothers had also chattered of baseball and "going swimming."

One hot summer day when she was about four, she tried to emulate them by taking off all her clothes and splashing happily in a mud puddle. Hauled out by a horrified mother, she was scolded and spanked. But the boys had never been punished for "going swimming." The injustice of it rankled for over eighty years.

As little girls, my sister and I reverently handled the fragile dance cards she had saved, crowded with the names of young men long graduated and gone into the professions. We stared at fading photographs of boating parties and croquet games, trying to identify adults we now knew as "Uncle" this and "Auntie" that. Since we attended a girls' school, we secretly wondered how *we* would ever meet such hordes of eligible young men, who would dance with us, court us, and one day, happily, marry us.

But her wedding photograph is not that of a pert and pretty "college belle." In her high necked, long sleeved satin and tulle, she is a grave and beautiful bride. She has no idea of the difficulties that lie ahead, as she moves from the safety of the academic world to the uncertainties of the real one. But she will face them with intelligence and determination, as well as love and devotion.

Why is it always too late to learn about one's family?

I had a fragile scrapbook of faded clippings, which my mother long ago pasted on their now brown and brittle pages. They were characteristic of her day — Bible words of comfort, exhortations to self-improvement, bits of poetry. Their variety indicated wide and serious reading.

I also had eight china plates she painted, their flowers all but fragrant. I think she went to art school. Why don't I know where? She did attend Wellesley College for a year-and-a-half. But why did she not finish?

My mother, Annette Harris Pratt, on her wedding day, June 1898.

Her hands were both artistic and capable. They dutifully peeled potatoes, lovingly changed babies, and beautifully arranged flowers.

Long after I was grown, she once asked *me* these same why-didn't-I's. She had been talking about *her* parents. Prof. Harris had died when we three children were small; his death left us few memories; he hadn't related easily to small children. I was awed by his long white beard and longer morning prayers, when the family — including Mary Sullivan, but not the two younger children — knelt in front of the parlor chairs, as he praised and petitioned the God of his fathers, while I surreptitiously itched and wiggled.

Even as an adult, it was difficult for me to think of him as the child she was talking about, the twelfth in a frontier family in western New York state in the early 1800s. His older brothers hunted, fished and enjoyed the rough pleasures of frontier life. They teased and tormented the little last-born, who was quiet, undersized, and wanted only to go to school and learn to read, write and figure.

When he was only eight years old (he had told my mother) he realized he *understood* mathematics! From then on, he acted as teacher's aide to the harried young men who yearly tried to discipline and instruct boys often older and bigger than they.

Why, my mother wondered to me, had she not tried to learn more of his early years? All his later life he had never sought word of the family from which he had so gladly walked away.

So — why did I not ask *my* mother more about *her* life as daughter, wife? Would I have been given answers? I wonder. Her generation did not think it necessary or even proper to ''let it all hang out.''

I only know that, when my father was one of Prof. Harris's chemistry students, they met, fell passionately, permanently in love, and were married (after a three-year engagement) in the beautiful college chapel, long since torn down. She had five bridesmaids in long, white, ruffled tulle. It must have been quite a social event in that little college town in 1898.

As three babies followed swiftly, there was no dancing, no time for china painting. And when — more than once — Father's business ventures failed, she had to let go the ''hired girl'' and try to cope alone with the coal range, and the washtub full of children's shirts and drawers (pants was then deemed a slightly vulgar word), her own long, ruffled petticoats and nightgowns, and Father's underwear and nightshirts. His white shirts, with their separate stiffly starched collars, fastened with gold collar buttons, as well as sheets and towels, were bundled up and called for by the local laundry establishment.

Sometimes in the evenings, when she wasn't reading to us, she did exquisite embroidery. Daytimes, her foot-pedaled sewing machine constantly whirred and clicked, as she turned out little-girl ginghams — dresses, bloomers.

During those years she suffered, not infrequently, from migraine headaches, immobilizing her for a couple of days in a darkened room, and causing us three children to move quietly, speak softly, and try — ineptly — to be helpful.

The "migraine personality" is better understood today. She must always have been frustrated by all that didn't get done, by the lack of time for music and serious reading. She must also have been baffled and worried by Father's business failures. She was far more practical than he. Her own good, common sense must often have told her that his visions were too grandiose, his planning inadequate. But in those days wives were not supposed to have such knowledge and understanding.

If and when they disagreed, they kept their differences to themselves, presenting to us children the concept of adult certainty and unanimity. I had to learn (much later and not without bewilderment and heartache) that two people, deeply in love, could still disagree, and fling their differences in each other's faces... yet come together again in stronger desire, greater need — and acceptance, if not understanding.

Father bought our mother extravagant gifts. He always had fresh strawberries for her March 3 birthday, in a day when such were impossibly expensive. He gave her money whenever she asked for it — and often when she did not; told her to open charge accounts in the better Boston department stores, and buy whatever she thought she and the children needed.

But it never occurred to him to let her open her own checking account. In that, however, he was only following the practice of most men of his day, who were protecting their wives from the harsh realities of the marketplace.

When I was ten or eleven — long before antibiotics were dreamed of — he suffered an ear infection, which (improperly treated) developed into mastoiditis.

My memory sees him, his fever raging, trying to dress himself, to be taken (by train) to a Boston hospital; hanging on with his left hand to his tall chiffonier, while, with his right, he scrawled a check for Mother.

"It was for ONE THOUSAND DOLLARS!" she told me, years later. "I did not know what to do with it! Could there possibly be that much money in the bank? And if there weren't. . . What would become of you children? Of our family?"

OUR FAMILY! A cherished, inseparable entity. To "do things together as a family" was what mattered most. This was the foundation of our upbringing. To be told, when we were young, *"Our family doesn't do things like that!"* was a stinging rebuke.

Growing into adolescence, we might sometimes think it would be fun to spend Sunday afternoons in the homes of school friends. But Sundays were sacred to The Family, to doing things together. None of us wanted to stage a rending revolt.

In those early days of the twentieth century, weekend excursions were practically nonexistent. Businessmen and professionals, as well as day laborers, spent six-and-a-half days at work. With only Saturday afternoons for relaxation, train trips were impractical, and automobiles, at 25 miles an hour on narrow roads, not much better. Sundays were for church, and such social activities as were appropriate to the day's decorum.

Our family went to church together, sat together, walked home together. Home to a roast-and-potatoes-vegetable-and-dessert dinner, which Mother finished preparing, as soon as she had tied an apron over her "Sunday silk" — Sunday being "the Help's" day off. (When there was "the Help"!)

Summer Sundays we often picnicked. And if we didn't, Father led us on afternoon walks along country roads or through wildflower meadows, teaching us (without seeming to) to listen to birdsong and look for beauty. I still remember the excitement of finding *fringed gentians* — such a heavenly blue! — in a familiar meadow.

The summer after Grandma Harris's death (which we spent in Amherst, getting the home ready to sell), we children found a baby robin fallen from the nest. Nobody told us we should leave it alone, so we carried it home, put it in a shoe box lined with grass, and fed it chopped hard-boiled eggs and water from a medicine dropper. It should promptly have died, but it squawked and grew, developing strong legs on which it followed at our heels like a pup, always screeching for more to eat.

I remember a path through a meadow, the sun washing over the waving grass, and little grasshoppers darting up over Mother's billowing lawn skirt. We grabbed them in grubby fists, turned and shoved them down "Dixie's" throat, whereupon he would gulp, blink, shudder, and resume his running down the path behind us, hollering for more.

Later we carried him in a covered basket back on the train to Boston, and out by another train to Wellesley Hills. He seemed to adapt to his new surroundings, but turned independent in the early New England autumn, spending more and more time in the treetops, returning briefly late in the day, when Father came home and whistled and held up his hand.

The baby robin, "Dixie," sitting on a book which sister Betty is trying to read.

There came a day when he whistled in vain; when we no longer heard "Dixie's" strident notes. He must have followed his kind south. But what would happen in the spring? Would he return to Amherst or Wellesley Hills? And would we know?

Eating our dinner one April evening, we heard a different robin call — arrogant, demanding. We dropped our forks and dashed outside. A robin circled over our heads. Father whistled and held up his hand. The robin dropped lower, almost touched the outstretched fingers, then flew back up into a tree, scolding sharply.

He and a mate must have nested that spring in the neighborhood, for we often heard him. But he never again answered us. He now lived in a world of flight and freedom, while our feet walked the earth. The gap was not to be bridged.

His skies were not totally unfamiliar to us, however. Father knew the slow swing of the heavens from long hours on deck in his sailing ship days. On clear nights, he often took us outside to learn the simpler constellations, and to share his feelings and that of the Psalmist: "The heavens declare the glory of God."

"The Family" meant shared interests. They listened sympathetically to our daily chronicles of school frustrations or excitements. We demanded to know what they had to eat, and what were the ladies' dresses on the rare occasions when they went out without us. And we always ate breakfast (bacon-egg-and-muffins) and dinners together. Mother insisted on clean hands and combed hair for the latter; she, herself, changed her gingham "housedress" for a dark skirt and starched shirtwaist. And we did not start until Father had "asked the blessing."

"Our Family" was also a sort of secret society, with private passwords, jokes, double-meanings — the result, I am sure, of our parents' reading to us, writing to us — letters, when we were (rarely) away, illustrated by Father's animal sketches, and jingles when we were home, to push us, prod us, praise us. . .

We were pretty scornful of those who couldn't thus play with the English language — not that we ever thought of it that way. A young cousin, spending a holiday in our home, couldn't manage a place card rhyme for the dinner table. We were pitying. . .superior, and said to Mother, "Don't let's have her again!"

The games we played with our parents and each other, such as Parcheesi and checkers, did not involve expensive equipment. Later, they taught us adult card games, hearts and bridge. Harris played chess with his father, but Betty and I didn't meet that challenge. However, from babyhood up, we read or were read to.

Beatrix Potter's rabbit and mice tales became part of our own folklore. We went into the jungle with Father and Kipling's *Mowgli*, and sailed with him and Robert Louis Stevenson to *Treasure Island*.

Mother led us more gently into Frances Hodgson Burnett's *Secret Garden*, now become a Broadway musical, and the homes of the *Five Little Peppers* and *Little Women*. We listened, lying on our stomachs on the living room rug, drawing on cheap paper with soft pencils.

I doubt we missed much by not having TV's sophisticated spectacles to watch by ourselves. Listening to our parents' reading stimulated our imaginations to create our own pictures. And, listening, we came subtly to share *their* values — not those of Hollywood.

Our parents couldn't often afford the theatre, though they loved it and managed to take us when there was something suitable for children. We saw Shakespeare's *A Midsummer Night's Dream*, but I remember best Maude Adams in *Peter Pan* — the wonder of her flights above the stage, and the excitement of clapping desperately to save *Tinker Bell's* life!

Back home, we hung bed sheets for curtains, and invited our parents to watch us perform. We created our own dramas, acting out the prose and poetry we had listened to.

We rode with Paul Revere "through every Middlesex, village and farm," yelping — "The British are coming! The British are coming!" — down the hall and out the back door.

We followed "Stonewall" Jackson "Up through the meadows, rich with corn, Clear in the cool September morn." As the oldest, I claimed the title role of *Barbara Fritchie*, hanging over the porch railing to declaim "Shoot if you must this old gray head," to Betty, who — as the general — waved her stick sword, ordering the troops to fire. Harris, the youngest, trailed somewhere behind, dragging his toy gun. He had no speaking role. He was "the Army."

As far as I am concerned, an easy chair in front of the TV is a poor substitute for a hard, second-balcony seat in a New York theatre during the Golden Age of Broadway. Working on a New York newspaper after college, I managed to see a number of stars and hits — the Barrymores, the Lunts; and Helen Hayes in her first starring role — that poignant scene in front of the stage curtain, played with William Gillespie, as the daughter he might have had, in *Dear Brutus*.

We were in our 'teens before we even had a "Victrola." Characteristically, Father bought the family an expensive console type, and a handsome assortment of "Red Seal" opera records.

But years before that, a neighbor owned one of the early Victor "talking-machines" — the one with small cylinders, before the invention of the flat disc. When our mother took us with her to "call," we were graciously allowed to crank the machine and play the records in an adjoining room, while the ladies chatted in the parlor. The records were chiefly monologues:

"A leddy got on the car wid a little baby in her arms. She gives
the conductor a five-dollar bill. He gives her a look. 'Is that yer
smahlest?' sez he. 'Yis,' sez she, 'I'm on'y bin married a year!' "

We considered this excruciatingly entertaining and risqué humor,
chortling over it to each other. It wasn't long before we knew them
all by heart, and could entertain ourselves in dull moments by recit-
ing them to each other, doubling up with laughter.

I saw my first movie, when I was seven or eight and visiting my
Pratt grandparents in Elmira, New York. When Mother sometimes
reached her rope's end with three small children only a year and
a half apart, I would be sent there for a visit. I was the oldest, the
bossy one, ordering about the two younger, and then angrily resent-
ing their defensive alliance against me.

Grandma Pratt's small home was quiet, serene, disciplined, yet
warmly welcoming to a loved first grandchild. I did not like it when
she blew out the candle at bedtime, leaving me alone in what was
always the fearsome dark. But if I were "Grandpa's good little girl,"
I could sing along with him after supper. So, before the trip upstairs,
I curled in his lap, under the glow of the kerosene lamp, and we
sang *Annie Laurie, Suwannee River, Marching Through Georgia* and
Tenting Tonight on the Old Campground.

His generation had fought the Civil War, which — later in West
Virginia — I was to learn about from a different angle. But the music
still touches chords of memory of those quiet evenings of lamplight
and song.

Daytimes I was delighted to accompany him on his round of
errands, holding tightly to his left hand, while, in his right, he carried
his market basket. Once we detoured and went into the new moving
picture theatre, which had just opened up nearby.

That was the day of the silent screen. But there have always been
sound effects. When the inevitable gunfire erupted, I grabbed his
hand, pulling him from his seat and back down the aisle, while he
dragged his feet, held onto his derby, tut-tutted and now-nowed.

That must be why I always close my eyes and ears to violence
on the screen. And thus, see few movies nowadays.

Chapter 4
Newspaper Girl

Graduating from college in the year 1920 was the reason I walked so easily into my first job as a newspaper reporter.

For the first time ever — that November of 1920 — all women in the United States, age twenty-one or over, could vote in a national presidential election. So the city editor of the *Boston Traveler* decided to hire a girl to cover women's political activities. A serious, young, blond WASP, with her hair in a bun, was — like the eager women with their new political pretensions — something different in this Boston Irish setting.

I was told to sign my stuff "Nancy Colbert." It is evidence of my sheltered upbringing, that it was years before I knew why my good English yeoman surname of Pratt was not considered a suitable by-line.

Life in my long ago suburban Massachusetts had presented a safe and pleasant road to travel. I knew, from reading, that there existed not only rape and murder, disaster and death, but hypocrisy and heartache, alienation and adultery. But living in a close, warm family in a well-bred New England suburb of Boston, I heard little and saw less of such. We couldn't then, as now, see on television the battered bodies, hear the tortured sobs. When I became a reporter, right out of a girls' college, I was insulated and ignorant. But I was also curious and competitive.

Nancy Colbert and Margaret Pratt, however, were two very different young women. The latter was shy and fearful; the former thought nothing of walking down dark streets and knocking on strange doors. She was — gloriously in her eyes — a NEWSPAPER GIRL! And to such, nothing mattered but getting the story.

Before long, I was covering not only women's political meetings and candidates' wives' activities, but general news and special features.

31

Radios were new in 1920. Reporting one Monday for my assignment, I was told I was going to build a radio receiving set, in order to prove this was so easy that even a girl could do it. I took home the directions, bought the materials, and spent a week putting the wire coils and wooden pieces in their right places. (Someone with mechanical aptitude could have done it in two days.) But I had also to write directions that were clear and simple.

The *Traveler* published this as a series, and later printed it in pamphlet form. A radio buff in the office told me the set really worked. But broadcasting was also in its infancy. There wasn't much interesting to receive, so I didn't spend time listening... which is the way I feel today about most of what TV offers.

The murder cases and court trials I covered were real life dramas, not TV's opiates for boredom. One week I substituted for the reporter regularly assigned to the infamous Sacco-Vanzetti trial. I presume I did a competent job of covering the day-to-day testimony, but I had little understanding of the social ills involved, and it was years before I realized the immense drama of social injustice I had been witness to. I wish now my stories might have reflected that; I know they did not.

I commuted by train in company with suburban business and professional men; women on the train were mostly students or bargain-hunting matrons, heading for the Boston department stores.

I never got over the rising tide of excitement and anticipation as I entered the crowded, dirty newsroom — that I, so shy and sheltered, should be part of this male-dominated world of frenzied action and achievement. Greeted casually by shirt-sleeved newsmen, already pounding their typewriters, I would go to the city editor's desk to get my assignment. I did not talk much — I was afraid of revealing my ignorance of everything by asking questions.

I learned to walk (eventually with assurance) the then narrow, confusing streets of Boston, running down the facts, trying to get the interview; dashing back to type it out quickly at my own scarred and battered desk, yell "COPY," and know I had met my deadline.

Evenings I returned to the gracious comfort of my parents' home on a pleasant, tree-lined, suburban street.

The daily journey was between two such different worlds. As in our school days, my parents listened attentively as I sorted it all out in talk... But I don't remember asking *them* about *their* day!

MAKING A RADIO
SET AT HOME

By NANCY COLBERT
Boston Traveler Reporter

Although possessing no mechanical or radio knowledge, she built a set that receives broadcasts from stations as far away as 30 miles. Her story, clear and readable and minus technical terms, tells how any person, young or old, can make a radio set at little expense.

PRICE 35 CENTS

Cover of the brochure I wrote in 1921 when I was a reporter on the Boston Traveler, *to prove that making a workable radio receiving set was so simple even a girl could do it!*

I appreciate now how unusual they were for that day, in accepting — even approving — a daughter's taking less-traveled roads. Later, I also came to understand how Mother might always have longed to venture outside the home, even though cooking and sewing for a husband and children had brought her happiness. Fears of one sort or another had always nagged her. But she never wondered (aloud) why Betty and I didn't seek nice, safe, school teaching jobs.

I was a little too late in time to have marched in the early suffragette parades, but of course I was proud that women at last could vote, and I hoped we should all have equal opportunity. But now that I stop to think about it, this never meant — for me — doing the same things in the same way as men.

I doubt I would ever have insisted on going to VMI, and I *know* I would never have hired a lawyer to get a *daughter* into the Boy Scouts. "The Lord made Man," according to the Book of Genesis. And then He made Woman. Which would indicate He wanted differences.

The Democratic candidate for President of the United States was not scheduled to speak in Boston that fall, but his campaign train would be passing through. I was sent to board it and get an interview.

That interview in his stateroom had not progressed very far, when he put both arms on mine and said something about "little Nancy." At five feet six, I was possibly a trifle taller than he. So it seemed to me the interview was taking a very odd turn. What did this have to do with presidential politics? Or was I the subject of — *Mercy!* — *advances?*

I didn't know then — I really don't know now. But I do know now how *young* twenty-one years old was in 1920.

I also know I thanked him for the interview, ducked out the stateroom door and onto the train platform where the conductor was standing, and demanded that he stop the train and let me off.

We were grumbling slowly through the outskirts of Fitchburg. The conductor was startled. I said again:

"STOP THE TRAIN!"

His hand slowly went up and pulled the cord. The Presidential Special slowed, gasped, and ground to a stop. I swung off.

Whereupon it huffed, puffed, started to roll, picked up speed, and disappeared around a distant curve. I was left standing alone on a crossing, with no choice but to start walking back toward the city limits and a telephone.

My report to the city editor produced an editorial consultation at high levels, but my brief interview appeared as usual the next day under my by-line. And that is all I ever knew.

Two other women, as I remember, worked in my time on the *Boston Traveler* news staff: Mary, who was tough, middle-aged Boston Irish, knowing her way around police courts and ward politics; and Agnes, whom the nuns in her school days must have loved for her gentle manner and sound writing. She and I became friends, eventually admitting to a shared, hopeless passion for our tall, hawk-nosed city editor, who called forth complete loyalty from his staff, and of whom it was said — "he had never found a woman who was a good substitute for whiskey."

I knew almost nothing about either whiskey or men. I desperately wanted him to be aware of me, but other than as a good reporter, I was not quite sure. In my upbringing, romance led to the altar, and if I thought that far, I would have had to think — in Boston, and in the twenties — of the Pope! And that was difficult and distant. So I asked few questions, did what I was told, and wrote my heart out, no matter how difficult it was to dig out the facts, get the interview and meet my deadline — hoping that somehow I was making an impression.

Perhaps I was. A couple of years later, he made what must have been an unaccustomed trip out to the suburbs one mild September Saturday, to be a guest at my wedding.

I was married in the flower-filled sunroom of my parents' home. A school friend played the wedding march on the family piano as I came downstairs in my homemade bridal dress and veil. Afterwards, we all had supper in our big backyard. It was a small, warm, happy occasion, as I remember it. But at the time, I was conscious only of the tall, young New York newspaperman, who put the ring on my finger, and was impatient for us to get away.

Every young, would-be writer in the twenties dreamed of living and working in New York City. After two years on the *Traveler* and a brief stint on the *Albany Evening News*, I stuffed my clippings in a manila envelope and headed for what is now known as the "Big Apple".

Again I was lucky. After an interview with City Editor James W. Barrett, I had a job and a desk. My dream had come true! I was a reporter on *The New York World*. I moved in the company of Heywood Broun, FPA, Deems Taylor, Alexander Woollcott, Herbert Bayard Swope...

Well, not really. They did not know of my existence. A new reporter on the city staff did not keep company with editors and columnists at the Algonquin Round Table.

But recently, pasted in the back of Ishbel Ross's 1936 book, *Ladies of the Press* (so it had not been thrown out, as so much has been in 93 years), I found a letter written to me after I resigned from *The World*, when C.B. and I were engaged to be married. It was typed but not dictated, and it read:

> "I am sorry that you have been called away from *The World*, for during your entire stay here your work has been marked by intelligence, fidelity and distinction. You won a high place both because of your personality and your professional equipment. Whenever you wish to return, be sure that we shall be glad to have you back." It was signed — in red pencil — "Always with best wishes, Herbert Bayard Swope."

Every day I rode the subway downtown from my rooming house, which was quite different from my Wellesley Hills home. I shared a bath with four strangers. The small, over-furnished room looked out on 14th Street traffic. I paid for it out of my $25-a-week salary. I was not bothered by the shabbiness, the inconveniences. I was on my own — and on my way — in New York City.

Actually, I did once meet Heywood Broun and his wife. I had been warned that she wanted to be addressed — not as Mrs. Broun, but as Miss Hale — for Ruth Hale was a leader in the fight for a woman's right to keep her own name. Of course, the first thing I said (appalled at hearing myself) was — "How do you do, Mrs. Broun?"

World City Editor Barrett seemed brusque and aloof to the new girl reporter, trying to hide her uncertainties. I never felt I knew him. When — a few years later — *The World* was sold, and that great, fighting, liberal, brilliant purveyor of news, wit, comment and opinion went out of existence one tragic night, Barrett wrote the passionate, bitter account of its demise in *The World, The Flesh and the Messers Pulitzer*. I wish I could have told him how much I admired it and him. But by then, we had all dispersed in different directions to other lives.

News in those years — so soon after they had received the vote — was seen to be what women were thinking about men's traditional activities, particularly sports events, which had always been considered strictly male territory.

The young and proper Bostonian (although by then the hair had been "bobbed") was handed tickets for the best seats at major sports events, so that she could do a woman's-point-of-view story on what happened on the baseball field or in the sports arena.

Thus, I saw Babe Ruth hit a home run in the 1923 World Series, and I had a ringside seat at the Dempsey-Firpo fight — the Champion challenged by the "Wild Bull of the Pampas."

That was the only time in my newspaper years that I was really frightened.

As I found my seat that night, I was unexpectedly conscious of curious, not quite hostile looks from the rows and rows of men above and on all sides of me. If there were other women spectators there, I did not see them. Further along my row I noticed a young uniformed policeman, looking at me with some concern. Instantly, I felt more comfortable; he would be there, if I needed help.

But why was I feeling I might need help? I was a reporter, covering a story for *The New York World*...No! I was a solitary swimmer in a dark ocean about to be swept by a violent storm. Unexpectedly, I saw myself as a woman alone in a crowd of men, frantic for the release of violence.

It came.

The bell clanged, the fighters charged. The shouting surged around and over me, rising menacingly with the savage ritual in the glaring white ring below. The roar beat against me. Dempsey knocked Firpo out of the ring — the roar crescendoed. Firpo climbed back in. The screaming was a knife.

I looked for the young policeman. He was standing on his seat, holding the head of the man next to him against his chest and beating on it with his fist.

I thought — I better get out of here!

Stumbling, dodging, ducking — but unhindered because of the mesmerism of the ring's violence — I struggled to the aisle. I tried to find an exit, panic rising in the face of closed doors. One yielded; the roaring suddenly lessened. Then I was outside, breathing fresh air, in the calm glow of street lights, the steady purr of traffic —

quiet people going quietly about their business. People, not a mob! I had just seen a crowd of people turn into a mob, and it had been frightening. I took a deep breath — and the subway back downtown — to try to put into words what the sight and sound and smell of violence does to men.

Frank Sullivan's humorous stories were a feature of *The World's* front pages. Two young women in Greenwich Village had an idea for an escort service, where lonely and quite honorable young men from out-of-town could meet and dine or dance with lonely, but quite respectable, young women in the lonely (and not always understanding) city of New York. Posing as just this sort of young man, Sullivan took one of the young ladies out to dinner for an evening of good food and pleasant conversation.

His story, the next day, was a characteristically entertaining front page feature. So the editors decided on a follow-up by a girl reporter, posing as the respectable young woman available for a proper evening out. This time the proprietors of the escort service had to know that I was a reporter. But they had been pleased by Sullivan's story, and were willing to go along.

So I showed up at the stated time, wearing my best navy blue and a new (rare extravagance!) hat, to wait for the nice young man from Chicago to claim my company for dinner and the theatre.

I waited. Getting hungry...a little apprehensive...regretting the cost of the hat. At last, the door bell rang.

It was not the man from Chicago. It was a tall, young reporter from *The New York World.*

"The city editor wants me to bring you back to the office," he said. "They're afraid something might happen to you".

I was indignant.

"I'm a REPORTER! I won't be hauled off a story like this. I can take care of myself. I'm not coming with you!"

He was quiet. Very polite — but very firm.

"I know — I do understand — I'm sorry... But you have to come back with me."

I was angry. I was disappointed. I regretted the cost of the hat. And I hadn't had anything to eat.

"I'm hungry!" I heard myself wailing.

"I can't afford a fancy restaurant. But we could get something to eat at Childs — if that's all right with you?"

Childs! Like hundreds of other landmarks of other years, it no longer exists — the white tiles, white tables, crockery, floor, lighting. . .spotless, sanitary, glaring. No romantic rendezvous, this; no candlelit table, no gourmet fare. . . But that's where it all started.

We ordered beef stew and talked about ourselves, of course. My reluctant rescuer had left West Virginia University in the middle of his second year, to join the then Air Corps. He had been waiting to ship out for France, when the Armistice ending World War I was signed. He was steered into newspaper work, because a girl friend had showed his letters to a playwright she knew.

Thus C.B. Allen had come to *The New York World* by way of the *Cincinnati Commercial-Tribune* from a little town in the West Virginia hills called Moorefield.

Chapter 5
"The Willows"

Kipling's cat "walked by himself and all places were alike to him."
Some people are like that. A house is a house is a house. History
— tradition — architecture — the quality known as charm — are
not as important as luxury bathrooms or a nearby golf course.

Then there are others, pulled by an invisible cord, linking mind
and heart to obscure and quiet spots all over the world. I once heard
of a woman who lived fifty pleasant years in the Midwest. Then
she visited the New England of her ancestors, and knew that, at
last, she had come home. She bought a shabby old Cape Cod style
house, sold her comfortable Indiana home by telephone — and never
went back.

Why do some places, and not others, exert that strange, strong
pull? And why do some people, and not others, feel that tug of the
heart, when they think of some croft or crossroads, some hidden
valley or sudden sight of the sea? Is it because the land that calls
to them was once toiled on, fought over?

I sat on a rock last summer, not far from the Minuteman statue
near "The rude bridge that arched the flood," in Concord, Massachusetts, while groups of sightseers surged quietly back and forth.
They were not raucous and rowdy, like Sunday tourists at some
resort. A guide in a Colonial uniform was followed respectfully by
small-fry. Men had died here, and for something more important
than oil. History's hand reached out and touched us. The land held
memories. Is that why we return to it?

C.B. Allen had lived in a Cincinnati boardinghouse and a Brooklyn
apartment; occupied a staff officer's bungalow on the African Gold
Coast, and built a home in the Jersey suburbs of New York. But
home was only, and always, in the South Branch Valley of West
Virginia. Home was in Moorefield, a little town that changed hands
thirteen times during the "War Between the States," and whose

41

population is still under three thousand. Home was a high house of weathered pink brick with a log and frame wing, near ancient willows on a stream bank.

I saw it for the first time shortly after we were married. There were rotten apples and evidences of rats in the big, high rooms; the lovely, carved woodwork was a dirty gray, the air musty. But the man's voice was warm with remembered happiness.

"All five of us boys used to climb on the big sofa in front of the fireplace winter evenings, while Dad read to us from the Henty books. I was the littlest, and I'd run last and 'split the middle!' "

"*Five boys!* It's a wonder this place is still standing!"

"Oh, that wasn't all — that doesn't count the cousins. Why we even had our own baseball nine! I remember once Tot's mother sent him up to borrow yeast from Cousin Sallie (that was *my* mother) so she could set rolls for supper — and he stayed three weeks."

"*Three weeks!*"

In my memories of an ordered childhood, a friend's spending the night was a planned occasion, carefully monitored by both mothers.

"Didn't anybody notice? And send him home?"

"I guess not. After all — one boy more or less — when there were always so many boys...nobody had time to bother...we had so much fun here... You know..." (a little wistfully, because it was such a preposterous notion for a young New York newspaperman).

"I've always thought...sometimes I'd like to own this place!"

Time seems to move more slowly in this West Virginia valley, set down between the Blue Ridge and the Alleghenies. Moorefield survived the quartering of Union troops during the Civil War, and had begun to feel almost as much a part of the United States as of the South by the end of World War II. In 1949 it took parking meters and a few votes for Wallace in its leisurely stride. In 1991 the parking meters are gone, trees have been replanted on Main Street, and, once again, talk is of our boys overseas. Only now it is in Middle Eastern places no one ever knew existed, in the forties, fifties and sixties.

At the close of the second world war, the old pink brick house looked very much as it had twenty years before. Only now, a man's long dream had come true. We owned it. The broken window glass was so many panes at so much per each that *we* must replace. It would be *our* job to cover the gray paint with white, to paper the big, high, square rooms — and to pay for it. *Our* hands would be blistered scything down and grubbing out the weeds and honeysuckle that had once been — and would again be — a lawn.

It had seemed like a splendid idea when we made this decision at the end of four years of war. The beloved boyhood home was up for sale. What better way to believe there was a future, than to buy it, and begin planning and hoping?

For me, there will always be the little hills around Amherst. If New England is in your blood, a bit of your heart will always call New England home. But, harried by wartime shortages and rationing, the prospect of having our own milk, meat and vegetables was an alluring mirage. To a "Retread," who had been sweating out wartime England, North Africa and the rat race of the Pentagon, the South Branch Valley was indeed the Promised Land.

The fact that Dad and Miss Annie had come to live with us in New Jersey was also a factor. That house had no downstairs bedroom, and Dad found even a short flight of stairs a tough haul, even with Miss Annie behind him to push a little and encourage a lot.

And he thought even less of New Jersey than he had of Kansas. Most of the time, he kept politely quiet about it. But we gathered that there were too many Republicans, and that the sun set in the wrong place.

Planning how to manage for them and ourselves, we had taken another look at the West Virginia property we'd acquired on war's rebound — 93 acres of land to reclaim, and an eleven-room house to repair. We'd tackled old houses before. We knew what it cost to repair a roof, to install a bathroom. We'd lived through that — not once but twice: the unforeseen delays and difficulties, the shock of the inevitable extras, the panic of a diminishing bank account, the deep excitement of a home taking shape.

Since C.B. would be leaving newspaper work for the executive echelons of the aircraft industry, and was going to have to be in both Baltimore and Washington, he thought weekly commuting to West Virginia was a good idea. And I thought — he wants to live at *The Willows*! We'll manage it. I can drive back and forth, too.

Some men need more room than others. When I had come to understand this, I could accept weekly commuting for both of us, and weekends of shared decisions and delights.

I recall a flight back to Washington from somewhere, a few years after his death. There had been desultory conversation with the Air Force colonel in the seat beside me, returning home after a week of staff meetings somewhere west. As the plane followed the Potomac in, his voice became warm and eager, and he leaned over to point to where his home was located. I sensed the work pressures slipping away, and the week's weariness dissolving in a rising tide of anticipation.

So that was how it must have been, I thought, glad that lights had always been on at *The Willows*, and dinner ready. And wondering if the colonel in the aisle seat would find the same.

Thus, in an atmosphere of returning hungrily to the freedom of the past, and planning, hopefully, for freedom in the future, we signed the contracts that would put bathrooms and oil heat inside the pink brick and whitewashed log walls, where slaves had once carried in water and firewood.

Inside a month, gossip had it that the number of baths was eight, but that is only normal exaggeration, and probably no more startling to some than the actual four — one on each floor and one for the hired man's use. The thousand-gallon oil tank was buried in the ground, and a neighbor from Ditch Hollow dropped by to ask (politely spitting out her snuff) how we were "a-goin' to git the faar down in that-air?"

When, to relatives and friends, we broke the news of our farewell to suburbia, some took it that we were turning our backs on civilization; others had read novels of the Old South.

"Ah — gracious living!" sighed a friend, picturing (doubtless) leisure and lavish hospitality. Neither she nor we could have visualized the combination dog pound, ag course, tourist-accommodated and gone-with-the-flood setup, which we, in those early years, dubbed Good Gracious living!

That first summer we hung an old hammock between the big spruces on the north side of the house, an ideal spot to relax, except that it turned out to be in the traffic pattern of plumbers, electricians, carpenters, painters and their necessary clutter.

In the city, Labor is spelled with a capital, is an impersonal force, subject to union regulations. In a small town, Labor is your friends and neighbors, and it seems unfeeling — on a hot day — to loll in a hammock, when it — they — are struggling with two-by-fours and BX cable.

The technicalities of jurisdiction did not unduly concern Hardy County. When the mason's wife was ill, the carpenter finished the bricklaying; the electrician helped out the plumber, and the paper-hanger's assistant was the town bootlegger. Later, the piano was tuned by a young man who remarked, on leaving:

"I don't suppose you need a dance orchestra?"

When I doubted we would — in the anywhere near future — his eyes fell on my gray and ungroomed permanent.

"Well, now, I also do a little barbering on the side," he offered.

In other days and places, construction delays were caused by one set of workmen having to wait on another. When a man failed to show up on our job, it was usually because he had to dig his potatoes or butcher a hog. A neighbor's roof was once left half off when the opening day of deer season sent every male over eight years of age heading up into the hills with a deer rifle.

There were fireplaces in nearly every room in the house, and I had always thought the height of luxury would be a bedroom fire-place with an easy chair beside it. An easy chair did, eventually, stand beside the fireplace in our bedroom at *The Willows* and, once in a while, a beagle would tiptoe upstairs and curl herself guiltily in it. But even on this amateur farm, it seemed as if everything was always happening except leisure.

That first May, Mr. Haggerty, of Purgitsville, delivered two little pigs. They reminded me of the old Lucky Strike ad — "so round, so firm, so fully packed."

"They're fine little pigs, Ma'am," Mr. Haggerty offered. "They're real nice little pigs. Why, they're jest as close to being purebred as any nice little pigs could be... And ain't."

We called them *Pork* and *Beans*, because this was our first spring on the farm, and we hadn't yet learned not to name animals we were going to eat. *Pork* was to be the hired man's due, while *Beans* would furnish our bacon. Her date at the community cannery, to become hams, chops and lard, arrived with late December rains, and the road too muddy for a truck to come in after her.

My sister, Betty, had been the one in our family who had wanted to live on a farm. She studied agriculture at Cornell, and after she was graduated with honors, having learned among other things how to dehorn calves, she went on the stage and married an actor. I was a thin, bookish child, with small aptitude for outdoor activities,

THE WILLOWS, Moorefield, West Virginia, in the 1950s-'60s after its restoration by the C.B. Allens. The "pink brick" house faces the South Fork of the South Branch of the Potomac River. (Photo by Bill Margerin, House and Garden Magazine, 1967)

and painfully timid about all animals. I had gone to Vassar and majored in English.

So now, in midweek, with C.B. in Baltimore, I was the one who had to figure out how to get the hog to the butcher. That was what always seemed to happen. No instructions, directions, no maps nor Blue Books had come with the farm.

"Do you think," I asked Henry, the hired man, as we contemplated *Beans*, all three hundred pounds of her lumbering along the fence, "that we could get her there in the Jeep?"

"I'll need help," Henry hazarded.

I rounded up a neighboring tenant-farmer, and then I stuck around, thinking I could help drive her. But you don't drive a hog up onto a Jeep! An hour later, she let herself be lured by a bait of corn and, as she inched over the edge, we flung ourselves against her hams and slammed the tailgate.

I thought that did it. We slipped a couple of boards between her and the seats, which the three of us (social distinctions erased in mud) were sharing, and headed down the lane.

But *Beans* would not stand for being bounced about in what she evidently considered a premature tin can, and tried to climb out over us. We fell out and beat her back.

I felt my presence an unwelcome restraint on the men's language — though not on the hog's. So I left the driving to Henry, the cussing to Kenny, and ran alongside, barking at intervals, like an excited collie dog:

"Watch her! WATCH HER! She's coming out the side!"

Gracious Living!

As for hospitality, it was warm but apt to be distracted. We loved having friends visit us in our new home, but at any particular time, we might be haying, getting stock to market, or coping with high water and the bridge washed out.

We had seven houseguests our first Christmas, and C.B. told them about the last Christmas the five boys spent there in the early years of the twentieth century.

"Dad let us raise ducks that year," he remembered, "and we sold them just before Christmas for a pretty good profit. We had more spending money than we usually had in a year's time.

"We all went down to Johnny McWhorter's store to buy Christmas presents, and after that, we still had money left. McWhorter had peanut candy — the crunchy, crumbly kind — at a nickle a pound. So we each bought five pounds of peanut candy.

"Then we remembered we hadn't bought a Christmas present for 'Mammy' Little. He was an old Confederate veteran who used to work for Dad, and he was always good to us boys. We couldn't think of anything nicer for 'Mammy' Little than five pounds of peanut candy.

"Could be we remembered he didn't have any teeth, and that we'd have his five pounds to fall back on when ours were gone. Anyway, that Christmas we took home *thirty pounds of peanut candy!* It must have been pretty near summer before Mother swept out the last crumb."

The unknown early settler, who built a cabin on the south bank of the South Fork of the South Branch of the Potomac River, had the ridge at his back, the stream in front, and fertile acres in between. The lack of a road didn't much concern him. Nor did it the original Randolph, who had built the big house of handmade brick, tacking it onto the cabin by a connecting pantry, when the Civil War and its aftermath of deprivation prevented him from building the back wing. He rode horseback in and out across the stream, and his servants brought in supplies by wagon. When the Fork was too high to ford, they waited till it went down again. When a road of sorts finally straggled out from town, it crossed other farms, wandering from side to side of the stream by way of half a dozen fords.

When we moved in, the place was reached by turning off the county road down a winding dirt lane, which ended on the bank of the Fork opposite the brick house. There, on a gravel flat in the sycamore shade, cars could be parked and their occupants would face the footbridge.

Two big logs, with a twelve-inch plank walk and wire handrail were anchored on each bank by a length of cable; the other ends rested on a concrete pier in — roughly — the center of the stream. When the water rose to where it flowed over the plank walk, the logs would float off the pier, folding back against each bank. When the Fork returned to normal, the bridge could be put back by a team of horses and a couple of good hands.

When the bridge was out, we used the "back way in" — a narrow lane between neighbors' cornfields and across their pastures, with six stops to open and close gates. Which one must NEVER fail to do.

Lost stock, broken friendships, and even lawsuits might otherwise result.

We knew all this when we bought the place. But we believed — too optimistically — that once we were settled in, we could persuade adjacent owners to join us in constructing a year-round road — or at least give us rights-of-way to do it ourselves. It was a shock to learn they would say *NO*, such was the local prejudice against letting anyone hold a scrap of paper which could be construed as a toehold on the land.

So, for nearly three years, we scarcely ever got up in the morning, or went to bed at night, without checking the color and flow of water in the stream.

When we signed the contracts for a door-to-door move from New Jersey to West Virginia, we were careful to tell the movers the truth: — that the house was located across a shallow stream at the end of a dirt road, which the van would have to negotiate. But city folks could not take such talk literally.

The stream was low that July of 1946, and the driver took the van down the narrow farm lane, through the Fork at a ford we had cleared, and up the opposite bank, because — once he started — there was no way to turn around and go back. When he pulled up at the door, he mopped his face, and asked if we didn't need a hired hand.

"If my boss ever finds out," he said, "where I took this baby, I'll be looking for another job. So maybe I better have one in sight!"

Miss Annie learned to walk the footbridge — she was always one to try anything — and it didn't bother Dad nearly as much as it worried us, because of his unsteady legs and poor eyesight.

"If I'm born to be hanged, I'll never git drownded," he'd say cheerfully. And as soon as he was safely across, he'd start telling us again about the time he took a horse and buggy up the river to get his sister, Mary, who had been teaching school in the country. Dad wanted to cross on the riffle, but Mary insisted it was better below. The stream deepened, the horse lay down, and water came in over their feet.

"Mary wanted to stick by the buggy," Dad would chuckle. "I told her in that case we'd both drown. She said — 'Well, I'm ready for heaven. I'm a Presbyterian and saved, but you're not!'

"So I had to drag her on the horse. Mrs. Lew Wilson and her girls, Laura and Kate, they stood out in water up to their chests an' got a-holt of Mary. After they got her out, she went and fainted! So I stuck her head in the river and that brought her 'round."

Putting the footbridge back was always entertaining for houseguests. We would wait impatiently, while the color of the stream changed from dirty yellow to gray to blue-green. Certain rocks would emerge, and the flow about the concrete pier would be noted. Then we would hunt up some of Dan's grandchildren down at the Ditch Hollow house, and ask them to get word to Dan up on the mountain. The following Saturday morning we would hear the rattle of his wagon, as it braked down the hillside, Dan walking alongside, holding the reins — a bent-backed, bowlegged little man of seventy-odd, who somehow managed to chew tobacco and spit, in spite of having no teeth.

"Well, Mr. Dan! And how are *you*?" — we followed the ritual.

"Well, it's like this now — I ain't so good," he would croak. "There's a kind of meesery in me back, an' I ain't got the stren'th or appetite, I useta."

All the while, he would be wrapping his feet in rags and stuffing them into a pair of rubber boots.

"Guess we ain't none of us as young as we useta be," he'd conclude cheerfully. "Quite a rain we had, wa'n't it? Figured you'd be wantin' us about now."

And off he would stomp, to unhitch the team and walk the horses down to the bank.

Putting the bridge back usually required not only Dan and his horses, but two of his dogs to run up and down the far bank and challenge our dogs, and a grandson or two to hold the staid and steady team.

C.B. would don *his* hip-boots, and wade out to the center, while Dan handled the horses from along the shallows. And the hired man would quit whatever he was doing, to cut poles, run errands and holler back and forth.

The horses would thrash about for a footing on the slippery river rock, the chains would slap and tighten, and — after what seemed a long time and a lot of yelling back and forth — the log would move slowly against the current and slide precariously up the sycamore pole and onto the concrete pier. At which point, everybody in the stream or on the bank would yell "WHOA!" — jerking the horses to a halt.

Then the watchers on the near bank would straggle up the path toward the house, confident that the bridge would be back in use before the day's end. When both logs finally rested again on the concrete pier, there were usually minor repairs to be made — putting in a new brace, splicing a splintered section of plank, tightening up the handrail. Then Dan would drive the team back to the barnyard, and be invited in for a drink.

"Don't mind if I do," he'd say. "Keeps th' chill away. You got better likker than most aroun' chere."

Seeing the stream for the first time, sparkling over wide shallow riffles between the high banks, no one could understand why we couldn't just build a better bridge a little higher. Only those who had seen how suddenly and frighteningly high the Fork could rise, could understand that "a better bridge" would just as easily be washed away — and cost a lot more to put back.

The contractor who was putting down our kitchen linoleum that first summer, stood on the footbridge at nine o'clock one warm August morning, noting the Fork was pretty low. It had been a real dry summer.

Fifteen minutes later the footbridge went out on a rolling brown flood of water, riding forty miles downstream after a violent thunderstorm the evening before in the mountain headwaters. Our entire construction crew was temporarily stranded.

Nevertheless, all those visiting us in the days to come, built us all kinds of bridges — conversationally. None, however, had any figures for flood levels or financing.

That was where matters stood on June 16, 1949.

*Moving van from New Jersey crossing the
South Fork near Moorefield.*

Putting back the footbridge. C.B. left; Mr. Dan right.

Chapter 6

Gone With The Flood

The electricity went off at 5:00 P.M., but there was nothing unusual about that. The REA had brought the advantages of *"The Electric,"* as locals termed it, to rural residents in our county. But the local cooperative was small, the lines often strung from trees, and the current was always going off when Miss Annie had bread in the oven, or I'd started a load in the washing machine.

But the lights stayed off and the rain kept falling, as it had all day. We weren't complaining. It had been dry for nearly six weeks, and the gardens and young corn badly needed the soaking they were getting.

Dad and Miss Annie went to bed at dark, and about nine, my mother (there on a visit) and I wound up a rather dull game of Scrabble, played by the light of the remaining kerosene lamp, and decided to follow their example. Presently the phone rang, and it was the REA's young lineman, checking to see if our current was back on.

"Maybe there's trouble in your transformer," he said, "I'll be right up."

Shortly the phone rang again, and his mother queried anxiously: "Has Junior got there yet? I'm worried. They say there's been a cloudburst at Franklin and water's running down the streets in Petersburg. Is the Fork raising? Is your bridge all right?"

I assured her the bridge was extra high and steady, since it had last been put back. I hadn't noticed the Fork up any at dark, but since the bridge light, of course, was out, I'd run down and hang a lantern at our end.

I threw a raincoat over pajamas and ran down the path. Suddenly, cold water sucked at my slippers. I flashed the lantern. The bridge was gone and the Fork over the bank!

Although that meant the stream must have risen four or five feet in two or three hours, I still didn't think it meant a flood. It was probably the first time since we moved there — the first time with water rising — that I didn't start mentally preparing for a flood.

Ever since coming to live on the banks of the South Fork, I'd heard about the floods that had swept the Valley. Dad dated everything from the Flood of '77. He did not remember figures; he'd been just a half-grown boy. What he did remember was that his sister had told him, when he came downstairs after daylight, to get the stove hot, so she could bake biscuits for breakfast. The old tomcat had spent the night in the warm oven, and he was still there when the kindling began to blaze.

"I didn't open the oven door when I started the fire," Dad always continued. "So then I took two buckets and went outside for water, and I saw what I thought was an awful thick fog. Jest about the time I realized it was water, I seen a log house float right over the mill dam, with a lamp still a-settin' on the table and a-burnin'. We found out later there'd been a Neegra family livin' in it, and when the water reached the second floor, the man, he tore up the floor boards an' laid 'em from the winda-sill a-cross't to the bank, and they all got out that'a way.

"The cat? Well now, he was a-makin' quite a ruckus, when I got back with the water for Alice. I opened the stove door and he went out'a there a-screechin' like the devil himself. He never come back in the kitchen after that."

While others chattered about high water, Dad would sit quietly, his elbows on the chair arms, bringing together the fingertips of both hands — his boney, old man's hands, with the paper-thin skin, hands which once had butchered a steer, guided a plow or gentled a baby; but good for little now. Then he'd look up — "I ever tell you about the Flood of '77? Alice sent me after stove wood..."

So I knew — one day — there'd be a flood. Whenever late snows, melting in the mountains, sent green water foaming over the gravel, I'd fill pails and pots and the bathrubs with water, so we'd have what was needed for drinking, washing, toilet flushing. And I'd be sure the five-gallon can of coal oil was full for lamps and the emergency kerosene cookstove. I knew some day we'd have a flood, and I was going to be ready.

But nobody thought of a flood in the middle of June, when there'd been no rain for six weeks, and the stunted corn, dry pastures and dusty gardens were crying for water.

However, there was something ominous about the way the Fork had risen so fast after dark — and those reports of high water south of us in the hills. So I set the alarm for a midnight check and went out alone on the lawn in the wet dark. Millions of fireflies were flickering above the flooded bottomlands. And the Fork was still rising!

I was down again, as dawn broke, and now I saw the flood water lapping at the yard gate, where it had never been before. Out in midstream, great logs rolled swiftly by, and farm gates and chicken-coops, and something that looked like a calf. They were seen for a second, then gone, the brown water rushing them past in a strange, waiting stillness.

There was no noise to herald the flood's crest. But the eddying brown backwater suddenly started to climb the yard steps; a yellow wave flung itself over the high bank on the opposite side, and a wall of water followed it. The river poured into the barnyard. I turned, yelling for Helen and Lenard, our current help, and they came downstairs on the run.

We dragged open the gate to the hog lot, and yelled at the old sow to come through; she was standing in water up to her nose. We waded in, felt for footing behind her and pushed her with all our strength toward the open gate and higher ground.

"Did you see my old white hen?" Helen called.

The white hen and the red rooster had always roosted side by side on the board fence around the hog lot.

"Yes!" I called back. "Her head was just above water, but I couldn't reach her!"

Helen dragged herself up on the fence and plunged into the water on the other side. She came up with the white hen, and we put her in the granary, where we had flung the young chickens. When we went back — much later — she'd laid an egg! Gratitude, we decided.

We ran the two cows and the black mare through the gates to the upper pasture, and put up the bars. We carried a calf and half a dozen shoats to the barn and shut them in.

The water was halfway up the front yard. If it reached the house, we could take to the ridge behind. But before that might have to be considered, I wanted hot coffee. And it suddenly occurred to me to wonder if my mother and Dad and Miss Annie were awake and worrying. They were up and dressed and at the windows.

"Does it do this often?" my mother asked apprehensively.

"Maggie! I ever tell you about the Flood of '77?" Dad began, but for once, Miss Annie interrupted him.

"Oh Will! — LOOK! Somebody's chicken house! Oh, I hope they got the poor things out! And that great, big tree! What next? I'm afraid to look, but I can't stay away!"

We were all like that. It was impossible to pay attention to anything for more than a few minutes, before moving back to a window or out to the porch. There was no longer a stream, and banks and fields beyond; there was a spreading, brown sea, with a cornfield drowning in it, and great trees struggling to stand fast. Water crept up the lawn, sucked at the edges of the garden. And from a gray overcast, rain continued to fall.

For two or three hours there was the telephone — at that time a local central office and a twelve-party line. Turn the crank and ask Central what she knew. But the girls there were asking *us* — how high was the water? — was it still rising? — did we need help?

C.B. was on two weeks' active duty with the Air Force Reserve at Mitchell Field, New York. The girls at Central promised, if he got through, to tell him what was happening, and that we were all right so far.

The flow was pounding into the opposite bank, and one by one the great elms began to sway and dip, finally settling into the flood, stately to the last — and taking the phone line down with them. One last, hurried try to tell the girls at Central what was happening, and then we were cut off from the world.

An eerie feeling. The whole town might wash away, and we wouldn't know it! Once a light plane flew slowly over. But we had no reason to try to signal, and it disappeared, zig-zagging low under the heavy skies.

It had been exciting during the day, when there were things to be done, and the relief of chatter, but when darkness fell — though the Fork had stopped rising and disaster no longer threatened — it was dreary, depressing, and strangely lonely.

"You done the best you could about everything. Now go to bed and don't worry," counseled Miss Annie, as she carried off their lamp, steering Dad ahead of her. And if all this was strange and somewhat frightening to my town-bred mother from suburban Massachusetts, she would not add to my worries by saying so.

Come morning, the sun shone hotly over the muddy mess, where driftwood rested in young treetops. I started to walk down what had been our "back way out." There was no longer a lane. The flood had scooped out great gullies, or flung logs and rubble across it. In one place, it had vanished completely, and the stream blocked the way.

Our flood, with its spectacular damage, was on the front page of metropolitan dailies, and hundreds of sightseeing cars moved slowly down the damaged highways, viewing the wreckage and devastation, especially along the North Fork, where landslides had obliterated roads, divided farms and changed the river course. But it was more than a year before we managed to see any of this ourselves.

Our own personal problems of getting to and from *The Willows* were no longer a joke, a gag, an occasional nuisance, but a matter of paramount concern, demanding a permanent solution. The Fork had changed its course. Could the footbridge have been put back, it would have spanned a gravel bar, instead of the pool in the sycamore shade, where we used to swim. And the lane on the opposite bank was mounded with four feet of gravel and windrows of dead trees.

Those first few days, Dan Cook drove his team and wagon down from the hills and brought us back from town a load of stock feed and staples.

"Reckoned you all might need a little help," he had offered.

Then we located an old logging road back on the ridge, and it was just barely possible to maneuver the Jeep out over it.

Now we explored all the old angles we had so often considered and discarded, dismissing most again, and knowing — finally — it must be an all-weather road out over the ridge, where the Jeep had been dragging through mud holes.

There were weeks of negotiations with neighboring property owners, legal details, conferences, deeds to be sent to Oklahoma and Texas. And once, when it had seemed all set, somebody balked. Worry nagged us nights. Maybe it had all been a mistake — buying the place, coming down here to live, bringing the old folks.

But because there was nothing else to do, we went back to negotiating. . .waiting. . .worrying. . .agreeing to pay more. At last, in late November, all contracts were signed, and the bulldozer moved in.

It was a gray Saturday morning, two months later, when the contractor knocked at the door, and said — smiling —

"Looks like we're finally through".

"You mean the road is finished? *Really?* ALL DONE?"

"That's it!"

"You mean we can get in the car and drive all the way out over it right now?"

"You sure can!"

In the downstairs bedroom, Dad and Miss Annie were napping quietly. Sickness had struck, but not until we could cope with getting in doctors and nurses. (Hadn't Miss Annie always said, "Things don't ever git as bad as you think they're going' to."?)

C.B. started the car and we drove slowly down the new road, up over the ridge where the saplings had been pushed over and the stumps dynamited; through the boggy spots where the Jeep had stuck, now drained by culverts and filled with shale, down onto the county road and on down to the blacktop highway. There we turned around and drove the mile back.

Thus — quietly, without any cheers, fireworks or champagne, but with overwhelming relief — we now had a way out and a road home.

When I took Dad and Miss Annie the news with their supper trays, I was remembering the Saturday afternoon, six months ago, when C.B. returned from his two weeks' tour of active duty. The '49 Flood was just one week behind us then. The Fork was almost back within banks, except that these — slowly emerging — were high where once they'd been low, and stone-heaped where trees had once stood in grass and flowers.

Muck and litter lay in windrows on the front lawn. We still had no phone service, but the electricity was back on, so we were cooking and washing without having to haul and boil water, and struggle with the kerosene stove. The sun was shining and the four of us were chatting on the porch, when C.B. strode in, his khakis muddy and wet from the five-mile walk out from town, across the water-logged and ruined cornfields and pastures.

We surrounded him with glad welcome; we drenched him with chatter — going all over it again — what had happened — what we'd done. After a while, it was time for Miss Annie and me to see about dinner, and Mother said she'd set the table.

Dad always liked a chance to have his son to himself, without feminine interruptions and fast chatter. C.B. lit his own cigarette and Dad's pipe, which usually took three matches, because Dad rather liked it gummy and foul. So, then they smoked quietly, and Dad asked the tall Air Force colonel how he'd made it home.

"The operator told me the phone was still out, so I just decided to walk it."

"You find the road in pretty bad shape, I guess?"

"Sure was — practically nothing left of it."

"Carl — I ever tell you about the Flood of '77?" Dad asked, after a bit.

"Well...perhaps..." C.B. answered gently.

Dad removed his pipe, which, as usual, wasn't drawing right, and studied it carefully. Then he looked up.

"Well, this was bigger," he said.

That was the last we ever heard of the '77 flood.

The footbridge, taken from the stream banks below The Willows, *with cars parked on the opposite bank.*

Chapter 7

Dogs and Other Dependents

The three Pratt children in Massachusetts had had a little black cocker spaniel called *Bunny*; the West Virginia boy had been companioned by a beloved hound named *Homer*. So, as soon as C.B. and I acquired a house and yard in New Jersey, we bought a beagle. When he was killed by a car one Sunday morning, we went back to the farm he'd come from, looking for another pup.

His sister was nursing her first litter, and the farmer said we could have our pick. We knelt to look and touch, and the thin little mother laid her head on C.B.'s knee, and said — with her big brown eyes and loving tongue —

"Take me with you! I know the hurt in your heart. Take me with you, and I'll make it up to you!"

It took argument, and more money than we'd planned, but Nellie rode home with us. She was a one-man dog, and she and her man had found each other.

Nothing separated them, until overseas orders came through in the summer of 1942 for the Air Force captain, stationed a year at Maxwell Field, Alabama. So, naturally, Nellie went along when we took off for his last leave in a borrowed Stinson 108, curled in her basket on top of our bags, stacked back of the passenger seat.

"You'll have to hang onto her on takeoff," C.B. said. "I'll be busy flying the plane."

She was wearing her leash, but — as he pushed open the throttle — I reached back and got a firm grip on her collar.

The yellow officers' quarters on the base flashed by; the wheels left the runway, and the nose swung northwest. The Nellie Beagle sat up, looked around and out the window. Her calm eyes and gently sniffing nose seemed to say — "Well, if this is the way you want to go, I guess it's all right with me." Whereupon she turned around three times, tucked herself into a tidy ball and went to sleep. Before

61

the first day's trip was over, she had learned — when the plane nosed down and the engine was throttled back — that it was time to stretch and await the landing. When takeoff time came, she would stand, tail wagging, to be lifted aboard.

Capt. C.B. Allen and the Nellie Beagle.

After that, there were thirteen long months when she sniffed less and less hopefully at every pair of khaki-clad legs she encountered; when she began to grow old, and the brown velvet of her ears was lightened with gray.

One day the khaki legs stood inside her front door, and she trotted over to sniff politely but without hope. Then her nose quivered, her tail fluttered, the sniffs became short and ecstatic. Another dog would have leaped up and down, but the Nellie Beagle was too old and her joy too deep. She sat back, lifted up her nose and cried. The colonel knelt beside her, and then the three of us were on the floor, crying together.

A friend, with her dog on leash, meeting her son at Dulles Airport, was stopped at the gate.

"Sorry, Ma'am. No dogs beyond this point."

"Hush!" She put her finger to her lips. "Don't tell her — she thinks she's people!" — and swept on through.

To Dad's way of thinking, dogs were farm animals, useful for hunting, driving cattle or keeping watch, but not belonging in the house. He tolerated (a little scornfully) our affection for them, ignoring their bids for attention. But once, when he did not hear me come in, the Nellie Beagle strolled over, and he reached down and stroked her gently for some time.

"Old lady," he murmured, "Old lady."

And the words ached with the loneliness of old age.

Now that I, too, am an old lady, with unsteady legs, fingers that fumble, and a slippery memory with names, I wish I had not always been so brisk and busy. I wish I had tried harder to be more patient and understanding, not only of him, but other elderly. I wish I had realized — one day I would be an Old Lady.

"Old folks live in the past," we hear. But now I understand it's not only pleasanter but we are trying to let the young know that we, too, once knew wonder and delight, and how it feels to "mount up with wings like eagles." We remember — we long to be part of it all again — but the tales emerge as tiresome prattle.

As Dad told his famous stories over and over, he must have realized that our laughter was not as hearty, our surprise not as evident, as once it had been. So he would make the climax even more startling.

When he was about fourteen, wiry, quick and strong for his age, he had grabbed a wounded deer by the horns and wrestled it down. But the time came when he claimed he had run down the deer and clubbed it to death with his Winchester, when he was only four years old! Even Miss Annie forgot herself and laughed. He was mightily offended.

"I guess I know how old I was. I was there, Annie. You wasn't!"

And he chewed his tobacco vigorously for a long time in dignified silence.

He found dog stories safer. The collie that Big Jim taught to chew tobacco, and the dog that bit the boy, Julian.

"It was Glen Spangler's very friendly little dog, an' Julian, he was awfu' ornery. He'd bully boys smaller than him, and he was always a-teasin' and a-hittin' at that little dog. And so, one day, he got bit. 'Twan't more'n a nip, an' he had it comin'. But his daddy, he got mad, an' he went around and got enough folks to sign a petition to shoot the dog. Jimmy Kleindienst — he was the town sergeant — he didn't want to shoot the dog, but he told Glen he'd have to do it.

"Glen said — 'You gimme one hour before you shoot my dog!'

"An' in an hour he got up another petition — with a lot more names on it — to shoot the boy!"

For a while, we had an outside dog, as well. Yellow Dog Dingo (Kipling, again) turned up, knew a good thing when he saw it, and stuck around. So we tried him out as a cattle dog. When he discovered he could round them up and bring them back to the barn by himself, he found it such fun that, several times a day, we would see them pounding up the lane, Yellow Dog Dingo gaily herding them past the porch toward the barn lot.

"In those days, our lives were full of other lives," writes Virginia Bell Dabney in her *Once There Was a Farm*. That was the way it was with us in those early years at *The Willows*.

Before we bought the place, Harry, Pauline and their brood had occupied the log end of the house. So they asked to rent from us a cabin at the lower end of the property, and Harry came up on his days off to work out his rent. A lean, quiet man in faded, patched blue, with a stubble of beard and kind eyes, he knew the routines of farm chores, and we could depend on him — except when he wanted to go fishing or get drunk. And he knew he could depend on us.

Their newest baby arrived one December day, and that night Miss Annie heard Harry's soft, anxious calling outside, and awakened me.

"Pauline's bad off," Harry said. "I want you should get the doctor."

She was, indeed, for she'd been hemorrhaging far too long. On the phone, the doctor said she'd have to be taken, as quickly as possible, to the hospital. But this was the winter before our road was built, and the ambulance could come only as far as the opposite bank of the Fork, which was running high with early snow water.

By lantern light, we laid a mattress and old quilts in the bed of the Jeep, lifted Pauline in, and I drove down to the ford, shifted into four-wheel drive and low gear, took a deep breath, and headed out through the swift, dark water — lapping at the blankets — toward the ambulance lights on the opposite bank.

Harry once traded a pretty good shotgun for Jimmy, who was reputed to be a good, all-purpose hunting dog. He wasn't much to look at, being a sort of fox terrier, with one blind eye and a gimpy back leg. But Jimmy would yip along a rabbit trail in the bottoms or yipe at a treed squirrel on the ridges, and I'm sure he would have tackled a bear with equal willingness. His was a very gallant spirit.

He moved down to the Ditch Hollow house with Harry and Pauline, but to him, also, *The Willows* was home. No matter how long he was tied, when loosed, he headed straight back up the lane.

We tried ignoring the way he curled himself into a tight and shivering ball to sleep on the windswept porch. Jimmy could take it, but we couldn't. So, shortly, he had a box lined with feed sacks and breakfast with the beagles. He repaid us by defending the place with shrill barking, and by bringing dead groundhogs and 'possoms to our back door.

Harry, understandably, got tired of owning a dog that was never around, and sold Jimmy to someone across the Fork. The new owner, too, must have kept him tied for long intervals, for weeks would go by. Then, one morning, he would be waiting on the porch, his good eye beaming, his tail stump beating the boards.

Spring rains sent the Fork ripping down from the hills. The footbridge washed out, and we were once again Jeeping across lots, opening and closing six gates on the way to town. Long before dawn a little dog yapped insistently in the distance, and daylight disclosed Jimmy, running up and down the opposite bank, trying to cross to us. It seemed impossible he couldn't realize the swollen stream was an impassable barrier. But all day he barked at the torrent, trotting miles up and down the bank to find a crossing; sometimes heading out into the flood, only to haul himself out again on the bank.

The next morning he was still taking it, but we couldn't. I headed the Jeep down the back way out, through the six gates and out from town, almost completing a circle, to the opposite bank, where Jimmy was dragging himself once more up out of the icy water. I brought him home, and Miss Annie fed him hot milk, laced with Dad's whiskey, and we wrapped him in an old blanket, till he quit shivering. Like others, Jimmy had depended on us and we had not failed him.

Our plans for the place had included a live-in farmhand. We had thought the kitchen sink and upstairs bathroom in the new addition would be quite an inducement to folks who'd had to put up with pumps and privies. We were surprised, however, to learn that what folks hadn't had, they hadn't missed! We finally hired Henry, a World War II veteran, undersized and closemouthed.

"There's only me and my wife," he had said. But when they moved in, it was obvious they would very soon be three.

I assumed, city gal that I was, that hospital arrangements would have been made. But Sunday afternoon, Henry was knocking on our door, wanting us to call a doctor. Even I knew that doctors weren't likely to drive out in the country and walk the footbridge in the middle of February to deliver a baby.

But a 70-year-old Scotchman, who might have weighed 100 pounds in a fur ulster, said:

"Weel now, you call me when the labor pains are coming every five minutes, and I'll come."

It was a cold, quiet Sunday afternoon. The good doctor had attended Presbyterian preaching in the morning, and was enjoying the warm comfort of his home, when I called him again. I stood by while he made his examination.

"If you need help, I suppose we could try to find a nurse," I offered, without much confidence.

"Nooo, it is not necessary; everything is quite normal." And then, looking at me directly, "If you will assist me . . . ?"

I had one 500-hour stripe on my wartime Nurse's Aide uniform. I was used to bedpans, and had learned what to do with a routine post-op coming out of ether. But aides entered the maternity ward in the New Jersey hospital — where I had worked evenings during the war years — only to wheel babies from the nursery to the bedside. The rest of the business was considered much too sterile and professional for us. Because of my full-time school teaching job, I had missed a required movie on childbirth, but one of the other aides had told me how ill she became watching it. I could only hope I could take the real thing without failing the little doctor who was helping us all out.

As nature took its course, there was no time to be sick. I never knew childbirthing was so strenuous! The doctor showed me how to drop chloroform on the cone and hold it over her nose at the proper time. But that took two hands, and I needed two more to hold down her thrashing arms and legs! I did have a moment of wondering what my former New Jersey hospital would have thought of this whole performance.

The little doctor worked with the calmness of long-accustomed routine, offering encouragement, admonition and comment in his spare Scotch fashion. Suddenly, he was holding a crying baby! He handed him to me, and I had just about sense enough to wrap him in a blanket and take him downstairs, where Miss Annie washed and dressed him, as his father looked on, her old hands trembling a little with delight and long memories.

When I went back upstairs, the little Scotchman straightened his thin, tired shoulders.

"Meeses Allen, if you will clean up our patient, I weel go down and have a cup of tea."

I had never before been confronted with so much blood and disorder — and no starched professional to tell me what to do! But I went ahead with warm water, clean towels and sheets; and at last — taking off her cheap, tight pink rayon slip — I put a warm flannel nightgown of mine in its place, smoothed her hair and saw her drift off to sleep.

Our house had a new baby in it!

This was not just "lives touching" — this was a whole new life beginning! A cord had been cut and tied, and the act somehow seemed to bind us more closely to this house, this community — even to the world beyond our hills.

"Our" baby thrived. I gave his mother a carefully selected book on child care. She read a chapter or two, then told Miss Annie the book was "nuts."

"Them doctors don't want babies sleeping with their mommies and daddies! What do they know 'bout babies anyway?"

Over the years I had seen friends tense and worried with their new babies, hassled with their care and an exacting routine. Louise kept him fairly clean; when he wasn't sleeping, she toted him around, jounced him, bounced him, gurgled at him; teased him, squeezed him; took him up when they got out of bed in the morning, kept him up till they were ready for bed at night; gave him her breast whenever he cried, and exclaimed adoringly, a hundred times a day — "Ain't he rotten, now!"

She also found it easier, in the summertime, to sit around in a skimpy, not-too-clean, one-piece "playsuit," chattering, and letting Dad and Miss Annie play with the baby, instead of tending to her own household chores. Dad had his own ideas of what constituted proper dressing for young women. Eyeing her disapprovingly, he would say — in the 90-degree heat — "I sh'd think you'd ketch cold, nekkid as you are!"

But Henry had problems, absconding once with the Jeep, and later getting jailed on an assault charge.

Miss Annie, who was, ordinarily, a most reasonable woman, became terribly upset over this.

"*Anybody*," she declared grimly, "that would keep the father of such a darling little innocent as this in jail. . .!"

We bailed Henry out, and got him admitted, on an emergency basis, to the Veterans' Hospital in Martinsburg, where (a few days later) he walked out and thumbed a ride home.

The State Police were concerned for our safety, and advised that Henry be given notice.

Dad and Miss Annie wept and hugged their "granbaby" — their "little tadpole"; Louise bawled; C.B. was grim and tight-mouthed, and I worried and talked too much . . . But families somehow survive upheavals.

Miss Annie said of Lenard, who followed Henry, that it looked like he was behind the door when the work was handed out, but he was nice to have around.

Tall, lank and cheerful, he flapped about the place, always courteous, always eager to drop whatever he was doing and try something else; always full of plausible theories as to why it would be bad to weed the garden today, and better to clean the chicken house *next* week. And he loved conversation! Once, when our car was in the shop, he drove a houseguest and myself to town out over our newly-built road.

"Do you ever see any deer here?" Clara asked me.

"Oh, my, yes!" Lenard answered quickly. "Lots'a deer — ever' time I come out. An' you know what? Right around this-yere curve, once't I seen bear tracks!"

"*Really?*"

"Yes, an' then I heerd somethin' behine th' truck, sorta growlin'-like. Boy! I wanta tell you — if I hadn't'a stepped on the exhilerator, I bet that bear'd'a clumb right in the back!"

There was no baby, when Helen and Lenard moved in. But there was an unending procession of pets on which affection was lavished, and, for which, rickety coops were hastily devised. Lenard was gentle with animals (which we liked) and almost succeeded in making a pet of a rangy, part-Brahma heifer he named Pansy, which we gave him in lieu of the raise he really didn't rate.

When he came to work for us, he had pushed the remains of an old Buick onto the place. He still owed fifty or sixty dollars on it, and was about to lose it, so we agreed to advance him the money against his wages. But before the loan was paid off, Lenard had traded three more times; for an old Ford, for a less ancient Chevvie, and finally, for a pretty good pickup. The chattel mortgage (meant to impress him) never caught up with the deals, so that was wasted expense. But in time, Lenard paid back the loan and other advances for things he thought they needed.

I finally offered a word of advice about too much installment debt, and Lenard promptly agreed such was unsound.

"There's jest on'y one more thing I'm a-goin' in debt fer," he explained with his ingenuous smile, "An' that's'a place'a my own. I'm bound to have me some land."

He had it picked out — five acres of mountainside. All he needed was $140. He expected the bank to make him a loan, but returned from town, surprised and disheartened.

"They didn't see fitten to lemme have it," he reported. "Told me I didn't have *security*! I offered 'em the pickup — hit's more'n half paid fer — an' Pansy — an' my *git*-tar, the new one — but they said that warn't *security*!"

They were both so upset that, remembering how it felt to want a place of one's own, we loaned the money. By selling Pansy and the *git*-tar, Lenard raised enough to buy some secondhand lumber. And then, in his spare time, he set about building a house. According to the U.S. Government, he was a carpenter.

We had early tried to get him on the Veterans' Farm Training program, set up after World War II, but our careful plans for bringing back our land hadn't fitted into the program's specifications, which seemed to be steering trainees mostly into the chicken business.

We were getting fairly fed up with bureaucratese, when Lenard one day draped himself over the kitchen counter and announced —

"Look! I think we-all bin gettin' a runaround on this-yere farm-trainin' thing. So I say, let's jes' ferget it. I can get in a class an' learn to be a carpenter four nights a week, an' they'll gimme fifty dollars a month. That ain't ninety, like the farm trainin' thing. But a little carpentering might come in handy, an' fifty looks better to me than nothin'. So, if hit's O.K. with you folks, I'll fergit about the farm trainin' an' sign up to be a carpenter."

At the end of six months, he had made a lawn chair, a plant stand and a bird feeder. About then, he quit.

"I ain't learnin' much," he said (the understatement of the year). "You stand around an' wait fer lumber, an' they don't tell you nothin' except hit's wrong. I'm a-gonna need all my spare time to build me my own house."

We tried to get him to stay on a while, save some money, and build soundly. But what he thought was freedom was the only thing on his mind.

"Too many of them are like that," our county agent shook his head, when we let him know we would be looking for another hand.

"They want to own land, and that's a good and honest goal, but they don't use good judgment. They don't have equipment, and they don't have any idea what it takes to farm!"

Perhaps I hadn't either, when we moved to those 93 acres. But I was learning.

So Lenard left. But the day came — much later — when the Snyders moved in, and from then until the day when age pushed the decision to move from ninety acres to five, we knew what it meant to have things done right.

Chapter 8

The War Years

Operations Officer, Capt. C.B. Allen, Maxwell Field, Ala. 1941-1942.

"This is different from our war!" my niece exclaimed over the long distance telephone in January 1991.

"Our" war was 1941-44. She was fifteen then; she is now a grandmother. C.B. was overseas, first with the 8th Air Force, then with the Air Transport Command, and I was back in our New Jersey home, teaching 8th grade English.

Because there was no high school in the town where Nancy's parents lived, her wartime transportation problems, and my wartime aloneness were both eased by her spending the school year with me.

Fifty years later, we talked on the telephone about the difference between a war fought in sound and color in the livingroom, and one seen only in silent headlines in the newspaper.

In January 1991, we were flying with bomber pilots, watching their targets explode below, or staring at their bruised faces, when paraded — captive — before enemy cameras. We were seeing the tear-filled eyes and hearing the rending sobs of women we never knew, in places we never heard of. We were being informed about support groups, and advised what to tell the children.

In "our" war, we cried alone and coped alone with wartime living and loneliness — and with wartime problems of rationed meat, sugar, gasoline... We knew our sons and husbands were overseas, but we never saw on TV the trenches or tents they occupied, nor watched them talking to reporters and cameramen. We did not hear the guns, nor see the destruction, except in blurred, black-and-white newspaper photos.

When the Air Corps Reserves were ordered, in 1941, to report for active duty, I was happy to learn I would be able to join C.B. at Maxwell Field, Alabama. I looked forward to living in quarters on the base, close to his work, anticipating new experiences and new friends.

But in those early days of preparation for war, the Reserves — ordered to the Training Command from northern cities and from various areas of civilian life — were not really welcomed into the stratified social order of what had been a choice Army post in the slow years since World War I.

The United States was painfully shifting gears to get on a wartime footing, but Reserve officers, newly arrived at Maxwell Field, were required to attend lectures on etiquette. The wife of another Reserve officer advised me against playing bridge unless I wanted to risk being snubbed or losing more money than I could afford.

But then — I was never asked to play. I was not asked anywhere. There seemed no opportunity to make friends whom I could invite to our quarters for the informal entertaining we had always enjoyed doing.

But I realized C.B. was happy. He might joke, or sputter privately about the stuffier aspects of life on a military post, but the life itself became him. He was Operations Officer, and all the details of a job I could know nothing about, seemed to come naturally to him. He appeared to know no inadequacies, feel few frustrations.

New England Yankee that I was, I kept seeing him as the Confederate cavalry officer of another war and a different generation. Not that he was one of your professional Southerners; he never clapped when the band played *Dixie* (with little ear for music, he may not have recognized it!), but it was in his bearing, his quiet certainties. Being an outsider didn't bother him, as long as there were planes landing and taking off under his command.

But when Gen. Doolittle flew in one day to talk to Capt. Allen about joining his 8th Air Force staff, preparing for the invasion of North Africa, senior officers were suddenly interested in having him join them for lunch; junior officers wanted to be seen with him. He was quietly amused.

Christmas was coming, but there were no friends nor family to join in the planning. I was unhappy — and upset with myself for feeling thus — when this might be our last Christmas together.

Then the Japanese attacked Pearl Harbor.

Immediately, no one could leave the base without a special pass — and few passes were being issued. As did all the pilots, C.B. spent his nights in a hangar, sleeping under the wings of a training plane, ready for takeoff. Since few had any experience in night flying, and no destination seemed available or possible, he — characteristically — refused to worry about it. As aviation editor, a decade before, he had flown in the first passenger flights to Guam, to South America, to the Orient. He simply did not believe Maxwell Field would be a likely target for Japanese bombers! Nevertheless, orders were orders, and he returned to our quarters only for meals.

It was during this period — just before the holidays — when one of the airmen in his command sought C.B.'s help. He and his girl in Ohio had planned a Christmas Eve wedding in Alabama. He had talked to a minister, had reservations at a downtown hotel, and had been given 48 hours' leave. With the declaration of war, all leaves had been cancelled. . . But his fianceé was already on the train heading south!

As always, with the young men in his command, C.B. — the World War I "Retread" — was concerned and quietly helpful. The airman was given a four-hour pass — barely time to meet his girl's train, take her to the church for the ceremony, and return alone to the post. But C.B. also arranged for them quietly to spend their wedding night and Christmas day at our quarters, in spite of long-standing rules against "fraternization" between officers and enlisted men.

Now, as I went to check the guestroom and plan Christmas dinner, I was enveloped in warm, holiday happiness. It had been years since I had known the young delight of "going home for Christmas." Now, C.B. and I were providing the home in which a younger generation would find holiday warmth and welcome. They and we, of course, have gone our separate ways, but for fifty years, Christmas Eve has had the added dimension of their and our "anniversary."

When C.B. was buried one August day, following a brief heart attack, four retired Air Force colonels — once his war-time juniors and protegés — helped carry his coffin to the cemetery on the hill behind Moorefield, which looks both east and west to the mountains; where — in 1941 — he had told the then War Department, he wanted to be buried, rather than in Arlington.

After Doolittle's visit, and before the overseas orders came through, I met some former civilian wives who liked to play tennis; and C.B. brought luncheon guests back to our quarters at noon, both military and civilian, who had flown in for conferences. Finally, I ventured a small dinner party for C.B.'s commanding colonel and his wife.

Most of the wives on the post had "colored" help. I liked doing my own cooking. But when Romie came to the back door looking for, and obviously needing work, I thought — yes — it might be nice to have some help with the cleaning.

"Help" at home had always been white and usually Irish. The "colored" I knew were waiters, porters, small-time tradesmen. There had been only one or two black children in the public schools I attended, none in the private ones. I was totally unaware of race as a social concern or subject. The vision and eloquence of Martin Luther King were years in the future. Nor — in my safe, suburban life in Massachusetts and New Jersey — did I have any conception of the total ignorance and complete lack which, in Alabama in 1941, were Romie's background, and which accounted for the fact that she was not already employed in some officer's household.

She swept enthusiastically with a broom, scattering dust all over everything, and was amazed when I showed her how it should be guided into little piles and eased onto the dustpan. She left what passed for her shoes at the back door, and worked barefoot, her big feet slapping over the floors.

I bought her a pair of men's sneakers. (That was when sneakers were sneakers, not designer extravagances.) But, if I were not there, Romie would take them off and tie them round her waist. I bought her a blue and white cotton uniform. She was transported with delight and sneaked it home, whence it returned, smudged with children's sticky fingerprints.

So when it came to the buffet dinner, I did all the cooking. But Romie was so eager to have a part in this occasion, that I coached her carefully on how to pass the dessert.

When the time came, she stepped stiffly into the livingroom, carrying carefully, with both hands, a tray with dishes of ice cream. She spotted the colonel's wife, a luscious brunette in flame-colored chiffon. Approaching her from behind, and slapping her on her alluring rear, Romie shoved the tray at her —

"Have some ice cream, Honey! Ain't you got th' purtiest raid nightgown on!"

Back home in New Jersey, I hunted a job. A few years before, we had bought a run-down farmhouse and six acres of land, on a dirt road (today — a four-lane highway!) just across the line from suburbia into the countryside. C.B. wanted to think of me there, with the garden and the beagles, when he was on the other side of the world. So that, and the difficulties of wartime transportation into and out of the city, ruled out a New York job.

Teachers were in short supply, so — on the strength of my Vassar BA — I was hired by the Madison, New Jersey high school, to teach 8th grade English, provided I would take a couple of summer courses at Columbia University on *how to teach*.

I was in my forties, twice the age of my Columbia classmates. The professors told us how children naturally love to learn; that all one had to do was spread before them the riches of literature, which they were eager to enjoy; that discipline was no problem, if children loved their teacher.

I believed every word of it!

Myself, I had never attended high school, nor junior high. I was the product of a girls' private school, and a prestigious women's college. In my parents' thinking, a first-class college education was the most important thing one could give a child. For some reason, they had not then thought that our local high school was doing a good enough job of preparing boys and girls for college, so they sent the three of us to excellent — expensive — private schools.

That we all received a first-class educational foundation goes without saying. But I sometimes wonder if I might not have learned earlier to cope with shyness, if I'd attended high school, instead of being a day-pupil at a girls' boarding school.

However. . . the fact was that, when I started teaching, I had no knowledge of public high schools, no idea of their daily routines, norms, resources, taboos; no notion what to expect from the pupils. I was an open invitation to disruption, disorder and disaster. As the newest teacher, I had the heaviest schedule, the worst classes. I was being thrown to the wolves. The kids sensed it immediately. I soon found it out.

It was a rough year, except for friendships with other teachers and support from the head of the English Department, and the school principal. Why, I don't know. Except that it was wartime, and they, too, had to make the best of what had been dealt them.

My "lesson plans" were rarely complete, and didn't work when they were. "Enrichment attempts," such as bringing in library books for a "free reading" period, fell flat. They did not *want* to read! What I had always taken for granted — reading for pleasure — they could not comprehend. Reading was *work* — to be avoided.

But I learned a lot that year — some about young adolescents, more about myself.

I learned, girls' school graduate that I was, that it was futile to attempt to explain the grammatical difference between the verbs *lay* and *lie*. *Lay* had only one connotation, and the mere mention of the word produced embarrassed giggles or explosive whoops. (I wonder if this is why most adults today — even those who went to college, even those who write books and articles — tend to use these verbs interchangeably and thus incorrectly?)

I learned how to relax quickly. I had to — to avoid physical collapse. During my one free period, I would rush to the women teachers' room, fling myself in exhaustion on the one, seedy sofa, drop off at once to sleep, and find myself swinging my feet to the floor, just as the next period bell clanged along the corridors.

I learned the distinctive public school smell. If I were suddenly blind and deaf, and found myself set down in a school hallway, I would not confuse it with a courtroom or cathedral!

I learned from a colleague with whom I usually shared a brown bag lunch (there was then no cafeteria) that cucumber slices on peanut butter make a good sandwich.

I learned (this had nothing to do with school teaching, as such, but with the lonely war years) to cook a good dinner for myself, and eat it properly on a plate, at a table — even when I was alone — even if I was tired. Which turned out to be excellent preparation for the long years of widowhood.

And lastly, I learned from an 8th grade boy, staying after school on a spring afternoon, what was wrong with my teaching.

"Staying after school" was such an exercise in futility! But it was the only permitted punishment for routine misbehavior. The teacher, of course, had to stay too, though she could use the time to correct papers. Halfway through a long and boring hour, with spring calling to us both from outside the windows, the thirteen-year-old suggested —

"Why don'cha quit bein' so nice to us, Mizallen? Why don'cha *make* us shuddup an' behave?"

"Tell me," I said, laying down my pencil.

"Oh, I dunno. Seems like you're tryin' to make us *like* you. Well, we do — I guess — kinda... But you oughta crack down on us!"

A light came on! Yes, of course I'd been thinking — if they like me — if they see I want to help them learn — then they'll try and pay attention... Only they hadn't.

Come April the school was still short-staffed, due to the war. I wasn't fired, as I'd half expected. I was asked to sign a contract for another year. I did. And the following September, I threw out all the Columbia maxims, so blindly accepted, and started to teach.

With authority came control, and with control, I could enjoy the kids and the classroom. With control and enjoyment, came confidence and competence. My sense of humor no longer expressed itself away from the classroom, in anguished jokes at my own expense, but in unexpected moments of shared laughter *in* class.

I found our family's old delight in playing with words, a useful classroom tool for making grammar understandable.

Yes, in those days, we diagrammed sentences. But when we took a simple word like *time*, and used it as a verb — a noun — an adjective — the exercise became a game, and sentence structure began to make some sense.

No, I never did try to straighten out *lay* and *lie*. But once, when trying to explain prepositions, I said —

"There's no such thing as *a behind!*" — we could all laugh uproariously together.

I found I loved teaching! I developed that sixth sense by which a teacher is able to spot trouble before it erupts. But there was very little trouble. We were friends. I no longer wondered if *they* liked *me*. I knew *I* liked *them!*

Multiple choice tests are popular, because they are easy to correct. But I never felt they helped teach 8th graders to read for comprehension or write with precision. So I made them write as often as possible, even just a paragraph or two — brief comments — their opinions — ideas — trying to pick subjects that would interest them. Once I said, "Write what you'd most like to do!"

The papers went into the wastebasket half a century ago, but I remember one well enough to reproduce it with reasonable accuracy. A pretty little blond fourteen-year-old wrote:

> "I'd like to be dancing all by myself on the stage at Radio City, in a long, flouncy white dress and slippers that laced up, and people clapping. The music would be playing and all the lights following me, as I danced across the stage.
> "And then again, I've always wanted to throw an egg into the electric fan."

When the war was over, and we began the thinking and planning that would lead to the move from New Jersey to West Virginia, I was genuinely sad that my school teaching days were over.

Five years after our move, my last class invited me back to their high school graduation. I went, of course, leaving the hills behind, driving north through Pennsylvania, and once again, the grim New Jersey Turnpike. They were no longer my junior highs. They were young adults, welcoming back an older adult, who had helped them grow up, and who had shared and enjoyed with them the give and take of the classroom learning experience.

Chapter 9

Books and Libraries

"It is a great thing to start life with books," once wrote Sir Arthur Conan Doyle.

I do not remember a time when I could not read, so I must have found out — early on — that books could provide information and entertainment much more reliably than dolls, games and other children; or by trying to frame questions that adults could understand and would answer. Books let me look at other lives, much more interesting, it seemed to me, than that led by a little girl such as I in the New England of 1905-15.

Our parents read to us, bought us books, and early introduced us to the local public library, where I became a bumblebee in a perennial border — flitting, tasting, sipping, sucking, wallowing — in whatever was on the shelves. I could become totally involved in the lives of heroines as diverse as those of Louisa May Alcott and Sir Walter Scott (does anyone today read him?). In my enthrallment with *Scottish Chiefs*, I tried reading it to the hired help in the kitchen. Norah had work to do there, and couldn't get away from me.

I was a painfully shy and timid child, and frustrated because I was always afraid — of dogs, boys, dark hallways, deep water, thunderstorms, being left alone . . . the list was endless. I struggled constantly to cope. Nightmares seared my sleep and shattered my parents' rest.

But reading eventually established the existence of two worlds — reality and make-believe. As I could move back and forth at will between books and my own little-girl life, I came to realize I could — when frightened — also exit dreamland. In the nightly panic of pursuit, I had only to STOP RUNNING, lie down, CLOSE my eyes! This would be wrenchingly difficult. But when I succeeded, my eyes would slowly open to my own dim bedroom, and — though my heart raced and pounded — I would know I was lying safely in my own warm bed.

It was my first experience at taking control.

All my life, books have "spoken to my condition," as the Quakers say. I read a sentence, a paragraph — and lights shine, bells ring! Turning the same pages, others are unmoved.

Kipling's *Mowgli* was told (in the *Jungle Books* which Father read to us) that — "A brave heart and a courteous tongue will carry thee far through the Jungle." I knew I could never be brave, but I also knew I could practice "a courteous tongue" in the jungle of grade school classrooms and playgrounds.

Nobody today ever heard of Hugh Walpole's *Fortitude*. But when one of the characters proclaimed — "It's not life that matters, but the courage you bring to it" — the words not only provided direction for the hero's life, but for mine as well. As with the early nightmares, I came to realize that — while I couldn't avoid being frightened, I could control my fears.

Long years later — suddenly widowed — I was to re-read E.B. White's *The Once and Future King*.

"The best thing for being sad..." — the words leaped out at me from the printed page. I was not only sad, I was lost and grieving... "The best thing for being sad is to learn something. You may grow old and trembling in your anatomies... you may miss your only love. There is only one thing for it then — to learn. That is the only thing which the mind can never exhaust, never alienate, never be tortured by, never fear or distrust, and never dream of regretting."

I had turned to my typewriter in those early days of grief and loneliness. To no avail. Perhaps it was because C.B. and I had shared our writing, been each other's commentator and critic, encouraged and needled each other. Whatever, I was finding it almost impossible even to write notes.

I had always wanted to learn to paint, but there had been no good reason to do so. College had fostered the writing; graduating, I figured that was how I could earn my living. But some fifty years later — following along with friends — I had joined an amateur oil painting class.

The woman who taught it was a splendid teacher with a great deal of natural talent — but no background of art training or even much education. Once I set up a still life to work from — the usual fruit, jug, wine bottle — but (I didn't know any better) all on a checkered tablecloth. Of course, when I came to paint the tablecloth, it refused to lie down! I knew there was such a thing as perspective, but I had no idea what to do about it.

"I'll show you!" our teacher said, taking the brush.

In a few minutes, the painted checks lay flat on the painted table.

"How did you know what to do?"

"I don't know — I just knew!"

But *I knew* this was something she or I or anybody could learn — from books, if not teachers.

I also knew that was what I needed — to learn something. I could try to find out about perspective and composition, and how to mix and apply colors — and whatever else I needed to *learn* about painting — instead of just copying pretty postcards. Learning was the road I must take through the desert waste of grieving.

I managed an introduction to a Washington portrait artist who taught a once-a-week class. I subscribed to an art magazine. I found out about art workshops and "painting vacations." It was exciting to set up my easel alongside students who could have been my grandchildren! During those strenuous, absorbing hours, there was no time to think about being old and alone. We were all struggling to paint the same model, suffering the same frustrations, achieving the same challenging breakthroughs.

"When the time of mourning is gone through . . . one is ready for the creative urge," writes the Quaker, John Youtblud.

So the time came, when — once again — I could write.

But of course, I had never stopped reading.

One of the first things I had done after we moved to Moorefield, was to hunt up the public library.

It says something about our town in the 1940s, that the key to the library hung handily just outside the door. The Library then was a room over the movie theatre, up a steep flight of stairs. Offering a few hundred used books, collected by the local Woman's Club, it was open only two hours once a week, so community clubs were welcome to meet there other evenings. The practice of leaving the key outside was discontinued only because harried ladies, locking up late, with a coffeepot in one hand, and half a pie in the other, found it easier to drop the key in a handbag, instead of hanging it back on the hook!

Money to buy books and pay someone fifty cents to sit at the desk from 6 to 8 P.M. Saturdays, dribbled in through solicitations and genteel "silver teas." The library's most desperate need was obviously a better location. But nothing else was available for the $20-a-month rent, paid — as their community service — by the local Lions Club.

"Why not build our own building?"

"*Build a building!* It's ridiculous to think you can raise money to build when you can't get enough to buy books," everyone said.

But what everyone doesn't understand is that it's always easier to do a big job than a little one.

The library had recently been willed $3,000 by one of its early devoted volunteers. So the first step was to buy a vacant old store building on a 40′×60′ lot, half a block from the center of town. The building project was presented to a town meeting as a matter of local pride, as well as the need for more library space. Years later we were to learn that we were the first small town in West Virginia to build its own library.

But nobody in town knew anything about building a library! Barns, homes, chicken houses — yes! But a *library?* We had no local architects, and no money to hire one from some city.

But a neighboring Virginia librarian was married to an architect, and he drew us some simple plans. The bank agreed to a loan. A committee member was in the plumbing and heating business. The School Superintendent, naturally, knew where and how to buy building supplies wholesale. And, as I had learned five years before, the carpenters, bricklayers and electricians weren't Labor; they were neighbors whose families would be using the new library.

And I saw to it that we had continuing publicity.

When I quit *The New York World* after C.B. and I were married, a newspaper-girl friend suggested me for a publicity job. She and I had become friends because we were each in love — with newspaper work, with New York City, and with our young husbands. Bella Cohen was small, dark, intense. The sheltered Bostonian blond was fascinated by her tales of escaping eastern Europe after the first world war with only the coat on her back. The coat was a Russian sable, in which she — like me — daily walked the streets of New York in order to save a subway nickle.

Those were the days when we all hoped — expected — to write the Great American novel — or play. Few succeeded. But Bella Cohen and Sam Spewack were two who did: many years later, *Kiss Me, Kate* became a famous Broadway hit.

As a publicity girl, I went to work at Democratic National Committee headquarters in New York, during Gov. Al Smith's campaign for the presidency; later I was with the Women's Organization for National Prohibition Reform, which worked for the repeal of the Volstead Act.

From that first decade of women's political equality, I remember three very different women. I didn't *know* any of them. They were the leaders in the limelight. I was just someone in the ranks, who could turn out good, fast copy, someone with a small flair for sensing the human interest angle in a news story.

Eleanor Roosevelt was not only involved in her husband's campaign for governor of New York, she was also active at National Democratic Committee headquarters. She worked hard; she was unfailingly courteous to the staff, but she never mingled with the ex-newspaper men and women used to the easy camaraderie of the city room. A certain distance was observed by all.

Belle Moskowitz was Gov. Smith's most trusted advisor; one rarely encountered her outside the inner offices. Heavy, homely, garbed in black, she was always a Presence. One sensed the brilliant analytical mind behind the brooding visage — and made one's comments brief. But she and the man she wanted to see President were both New Yorkers. They knew their city; they were acquainted with their state. They did not understand the great reach of rural America that lay beyond the Hudson River. Nor had the time yet come to elect a Catholic as President of the United States.

Mrs. Charles Sabin, who headed the Women's Organization for National Prohibition Reform was a banker's wife and fashionable socialite. She presided pleasantly. A thousand women delegates from all over the country felt more at ease, when she quipped — greeting them from the podium in a fashionable New York hotel —

"Here we all are, with victory in every heart, and a new navy blue spring print on every back!"

But hers did not come off a department store rack.

In the news, she was always referred to as; *Mrs. Charles* Sabin. I do not know whether that says something about her or her generation, or her family — or the years before World War II.

Thus, promoting the new Hardy County Public Library was not only a labor of love, but a chance to put to work for a cause and community I believed in, the skills I had learned in public relations jobs. From the cornerstone laying in June 1952 to the formal opening in October, the new library plans and progress were headlined weekly in the news.

"We'll invite the governor to dedicate it!"

"The *Governor?* What makes you think he'll come?"

"That's what governors are for!"

Everybody in town got into the act. Home gardeners provided late 'mums for decoration; the State Road Superintendent was an expert at garnishing a whole baked ham; the variety store manager furnished patriotic bunting with which the library ladies swathed the makeshift platform in front of the library. A grade school essay contest selected two children, one white, one black, to hold the ribbon across the new library door, to be cut by the library chairman.

But would there be a crowd?

The politician's dilemma was ours, and we used a politician's gimmick. We asked the School Superintendent if school couldn't be dismissed early, so that the school band could parade up Main Street.

As the VIP's stepped up to their places on the sidewalk platform, our band-uniformed boys and girls — beating and tootling — pivoted smartly at the town's one stoplight, and the trailing crowds swept in around them and the platform, to stand at attention for the *Star-Spangled Banner.*

The library's big day happened, that year, to be the opening day of West Virginia's squirrel hunting season. So the next day one New York newspaper carried a paragraph about West Virginia's governor throwing out the first squirrel at the library dedication! C.B. never admitted to being responsible.

To pay off our building debt (accomplished in seven years) we started an annual House & Garden Tour. These tours have continued for over thirty years as Hardy County's Heritage Weekend — promoting tourism, making us all realize the importance of conservation and preservation — and helping to balance the library budget.

Hardy County boasts some of the most spectacular scenery in the East. But it is split by a ridge of the Shenandoahs, so those living to the East could not easily get books in Moorefield, though we were calling ourselves a *county* library. So we tried setting up "book deposit stations" in community centers across the mountain — a church or a general store. But these small supplies of discards and duplicates were quickly exhausted.

*Costumed hostesses for Hardy County's annual HERITAGE WEEKEND,
a fund-raiser for the Library; taken at THE WILLOWS in the late 1950s.
(The photo is by the late Dave Cruise, State photographer; it appeared in
state publications and on West Virginia's official state highway map for
1960.)*

While serving a term on the State Library Commission, I learned about the state's bookmobile service in some rural areas. One of these early bookmobiles was about to be replaced, and we were allowed to buy it for $100. It was slow-moving, top-heavy and required double-clutching to get it over the mountains. We had no funds to pay a driver, so School Superintendent Dispanet (again to our rescue) excused a husky high school senior early on Tuesdays to drive our library workers on book delivery trips across the mountains.

His sons, who do not know the West Virginia hills, now have his Distinguished Service Medal, and the knowledge that he died a hero in Vietnam. I hope they also know that, as a teenager, he was a community volunteer. Of such satisfactions and sadnesses is small-town living.

After Bill was graduated, the School Board loaned us a part-time school bus driver.

"Buck" was proud of our "library on wheels." Parked next to a post office, he would hail passersby —

"Come on! Getta book! It ain't gonna hurt'cha!"

It was some time before we found out that — when he glanced at the menu at our quick lunch stops, threw it down and said, "Guess I'll have a hamburger and coffee" — he hadn't read it. He had never learned to read!

Today our library is actively involved in the country's literacy program, as volunteers take training and then — on a one-to-one basis — try to help middle-aged to elderly men and women master the skill that will enable them to read the Bible or shopping labels or get a truck driver's license.

Though there have been far too many such in our mountains, books and reading were important to Moorefield's earliest residents. Records in our archives show that a Literary Society was started in 1824.

One finds no women's names on the list of its first members. (There were no men's names on the first library board formed a hundred years later!) The earliest entry in the secretary's ledger (preserved in our library's extensive archives) reads:

"The subscribers, considering the benefits which will result from the establishment of a library facility, with which one might be associated, provided a number should associate together for such a purpose, have agreed and do hereby agree to advance one dollar each, as soon as a sufficient number of subscribers can be attained, the amount of which sum will immediately be applied to the purchase of the most useful works...''

There is no record of which were those "useful works," and subsequent minutes indicate some squabbling over whether or not dues and fines had been paid. But Moorefield thus had a hundred-year tradition of library need and use. So once there was established in town a bona fide, accessible little library, books and patrons multiplied. The library opened its doors *five days* a week. The town and county later acceded to requests for regular funding. And we kept up the publicity.

The Hardy County Public Library, in 1966, won the prestigious Dorothy Canfield Fisher Book-of-the-Month Club Award as one of the six best small libraries in the nation. The award was to be presented during National Library Week in April. An official luncheon was suggested for the occasion, with an author as speaker, and we were advised to make a big production out of it.

That was one bit of good advice we didn't need. From the minute we received news of the award, we went into high gear on arrangements. But there are always hitches, whether it's with the Queen of England in Washington, D.C. or with a Poultry Princess in Moorefield, WV!

Our largest local industry, a poultry processing plant, was planning to stage ground-breaking ceremonies for a new building on that same day. Since the Governor had already accepted *our* invitation, it was suggested that both affairs be combined.

I thought that, when we had a speaker such as Maurice Brooks, author of *The Appalachians*, we did not need a Miss Pinfeathers (so to speak) at the head table. And said so. Perhaps a little too emphatically.

Friends of both Culture and Industry solved the impasse by arranging for the Governor to wield the shovel at the poultry plant, and then lunch with the Literati! Peace prevailed.

The library had been built to house a possible collection of six thousand books. By the 1970s, we had over twelve thousand, crowded on the shelves, stacked on the floor. It was time to move again.

Fortunately, this was when federal as well as state funds were being made available for building public libraries. This time the unknown road we were to travel was one of government regulations, federal wage scales and matching grants. This was to be not only a community effort of fund-raising, but a government-supervised building program.

Again we remodeled an old store building — this time a large market at our Main Street stoplight. We had an out-of-state firm of architects, state engineers, and federal audits. But in spite — or because — of all this officialdom, the new library materialized in the center of town, and West Virginia's senior senator, then Majority Leader, Robert Byrd, flew in to dedicate our second Hardy County Public Library.

Two weeks before that, we had to move some fifteen thousand books. It was a distance of only one downhill block, but it was a problem of one day and one librarian.

That Saturday morning, the Hawse Supermarket loaned us half of its shopping carts. We had organized competing teams of high school students. Adult volunteers in the old library stacked the books by categories and loaded them in the shopping carts. Boys and girls raced down the sidewalk, halted at the stoplight, wheeled across Main Street, as the light turned green, and were met at the new library by other adult volunteers, who unloaded the books, shelved them in temporary order under the librarian's supervision, while the kids rushed back up the block for another load.

By noon we had transported all fifteen thousand books, and had distributed soft drinks to all, and prizes to the winning teams.

But, as a PR person, I had a frustrating disappointment.

I had arranged for someone to get some shots of all this. He was there with his camera when our volunteer traffic director held up a big, black hand to stop an enormous semi-trailer, so that a quite small girl could wheel her grocery cart, piled high with books, across the intersection on U.S. 220, directly in front of the towering, panting, interstate behemoth.

But my cameraman had forgotten to load film in his camera!

When, in the 1950s, I volunteered to work in the old Moorefield library up the long flight of stairs over the movie theatre, I had no idea where and how far the road of community service would lead both the library and me. Years later, when we were settled in our new, efficient, well-designed federally-built library at the stoplight, the West Virginia Library Association gave me its highest award for 31 years of outstanding library service.

Recognition is always pleasant, and by then I had pretty much forgotten all the difficulties and frustrations of those thirty-one years. But I shall never forget the friendships and the fun.

And then, in my eighties, there was one more job to do.

The muddy waters of the 1985 "500-year flood" stood four feet deep over the library's expensive new carpeting November 5 of that year. While we were cleaning up after the waters receded, we found there were no files, photos nor records documenting Moorefield's '49 flood. At the library, we resolved this must not be the case with the '85 disaster. We decided a film documentary of the event must be produced.

As with our first building, there was nobody who knew anything about such a project, though we *were* told the cost would be prohibitive. But we knew this was something that ought to be done, so we set about doing it.

A young West Virginia University graduate student in Communications answered our ad for a director. We hired her, and then found, also in Morgantown, two young women professionals to do the filming.

The Flood, the Rainbow, and the Olive Leaf, a half-hour documentary, had its first public showing at the library on the flood's anniversary, a year later. We had been given a $5,000 grant for the project by the State Humanities Council. It actually cost us seven thousand dollars and five cents and won us an award from the West Virginia Library Association.

This is the Hardy County Public Library's first bookmobile, parked at a country cross-roads, with high school senior Bill Denny, as driver. A few years later, as Capt. Denny, he died a hero, in Vietnam.

HARDY COUNTY PUBLIC LIBRARY
MOOREFIELD, WEST VIRGINIA

LUNCHEON PROGRAM

In Honor of the 1966 Book-of-the-Month Club Award—April 17, 1966, 1:30 P. M.

MOOREFIELD FIRE HALL

Welcome .... Mrs. J. W. Fisher, President
Hardy County Public Library

Invocation .... The Reverend Tennis E. Painter,
Duffey Memorial Methodist Church

Introduction of Guests .... Master of Ceremonies, Ralph J. Bean, Sr.
Former Library Board Member; Former
President West Virginia Senate

— *Speakers* —

Maurice Brooks, author of "The Appalachians" and Professor of Wildlife Manage-
ment, West Virginia University

The Honorable Hulett C. Smith, Governor of West Virginia

Presentation of the Award .... Mr. Campbell E. Beall, Martinsburg,
Member, West Virginia Library Commission

Acceptance .... Mrs. C. B. Allen, Former President of
the Hardy County Public Library

Invitation to Visit the Library .... Mrs. Roscoe Collins, Librarian

Benediction .... The Reverend Robert B. Woodworth
Moorefield Presbyterian Church

*The luncheon program in honor of the 1966 Book-of-the-Month Club
award to the Hardy County Public Library.*

Chapter 10
Sundays and Holidays

When we were children, growing up, the Bible had something to say to us, thanks to our parents. I am a little sad that doesn't seem to be true of the second and third generations. It's not a question of morals. It's the loss of a glory of language, of a majesty of conception, of a link, not only with our American past, but with Greek philosophy and Judeo-Christian beliefs, which have been basic to English thought and writing.

It sometimes seems as if we, in America, live today in a present of restless movement and endless consumption, like voracious caterpillars, crawling up and down a tree; to whom its roots — which anchor the soil — and its branches — which reach for the stars — mean nothing except the satisfaction of appetite.

(That's not very nice, is it? Language does sometimes carry one away!)

The English language is so magnificently full of precise and perfect words — to describe, explain, identify — that I have often sharply objected to the young of my acquaintance describing everything as either neat or shitty.

Language brings us back to the Bible, which was basic to my generation and to those preceding. I have my mother's Bible, dated 1869. The print is hard to read and the pages thinner than the skin on my 93-year-old hands. I also have *her* mother's Bible and Book of Common Prayer, with her name — *Ellen P. Harris* — stamped in gold on the cover.

Margaret Pratt is stamped in gold also, on the cover of the little Bible my parents gave me when I joined the First Congregational Church in Wellesley Hills. I had just turned sixteen — an infinitely younger and more unsophisticated sixteen than that age now implies. I wore my first *bought* trailored two-piece suit (Mother had always made all our dresses), which was not quite warm enough for the first of April in Massachusetts. But I was too pleased and proud to put my old winter coat on over it!

Who of my far-flung family today is going to be interested in *these* antiques? The empire mahogany table, the maple slant-top desk, the mahogany four-poster — yes! But the Bibles?. . . I wonder.

I'm not meaning to be critical. I'm just wondering about values.

I was introduced to "values" in my art workshops. I came slowly to see why some paintings — like mine — appeared flat and uninteresting, while others had depth and distinction. Lives are like that.

My Grandfather Pratt's Book of Psalms is incredibly worn — read — heavily annotated by his oldest daughter, my admired Auntie Anna, whose life and thinking offered directions I have not always chosen to follow.

I was trying, recently, to describe her, but she is not readily explicable in today's terms. Perspectives have changed. And again — there is so much I never thought to ask about.

Hundreds of young men never returned from the Civil War battlefields, leaving hundreds of young women, who might ordinarily have become wives and mothers, to seek and find other outlets for their caring and concern.

Whether or not this was her personal history, I do not know. But sometime, as a young woman, Anna Beach Pratt gave her life completely to God. Religious conversion is nothing new, then or now. Plenty profess to "find God" and lives are sometimes dramatically changed in the process.

For her — a Protestant — a Presbyterian — there was no obvious line to cross, no convent doors to open and close. She continued the role of dutiful daughter; at Elmira College (the first woman's college in America), she studied both the classics and the Bible. But she looked long and hard at the less fortunate young women in her city. She saw the complete lack of opportunity for education and social life in the lives of factory girls in Elmira, and she started a club to provide such opportunities.

Later, when she and others realized the duplication of effort by community agencies, they built the Federation Building, with offices, a cafeteria, all kinds of activities and Sunday afternoon gatherings for the exchange of religious views.

It was about this time that my father would have been having financial difficulties, so his parents sold their home to help him (moving to the little house I visited as a child), and Auntie Anna looked for a paying job.

"Overseer of the Poor" was the one she had in mind. But the city would not consider a *woman* for a public office. They appointed her father to the thousand-dollar-a-year job, and let her be book-keeper — at five dollars a week! But it was her father who kept the books; she did the investigating, the case work; she organized the reforms.

The generation gap makes it difficult really to understand another's life. I do know her faith was not a matter of church attendance and activities, nor even of a multiplicity of good works. There was about her a high serenity, a strong sense of trust — as of a loving daughter, holding her father's hand.

I have wanted all my life to follow in her footsteps of faith, but my feet have wandered. There were a few weeks of so-called "conversion," when I was quite young. I did a lot of what I thought was praying and Scripture reading — quite common for young girls in those days. My parents — no strangers to faith and good works — gently let me work through it. But, like most exercises in mental or physical health, they dwindled in urgency and effort. Life offered so many distractions, directions, ambitions, yearnings. I was never one to wait to be "led".

After her father's death, Auntie Anna moved her mother and herself to Philadelphia, where she received her graduate degree in social work from the University of Pennsylvania; later becoming head of the White-Williams Foundation, a social service agency, where she had great impact. After her death, the city of Philadelphia named a public school after her.

She had been brought up in the Presbyterian Church of her fathers, but — after moving to Philadelphia — became a member of the Society of Friends, the Quakers. Her religion had never been one of creeds and commandments, but of Listening for the Word, Waiting on the Lord. Such Quaker concepts, along with simplicity in lifestyle were already basic to her beliefs.

Living with someone to whom *things* mean little, can lead to family arguments. Grandma Pratt had her own ideas of what was fitting and proper. She couldn't see why Anna wouldn't buy herself a good, new, stylish suit, instead of always wearing dresses made by the sewing classes at the White-Williams Foundation.

The young are clothes conscious. But in my memory, she was always — queenly. A Presence — but a gentle and domestic one. I remember her evenings, carefully darning her black cotton stockings and gloves under the lamplight.

My Aunt Anna in her Germantown garden.

Working in New York, I was able to visit her several times in the Germantown home she shared with another woman, following Grandma Pratt's death. Beauty, order and peace dwelt there with the family mahogany, the old Orential rugs, and in the lovely little garden to the rear. She took pleasure in small ceremonies, such as making and serving strong, black, after-dinner Turkish coffee, with the brass service she had brought back from a trip to the Far East. When she traveled, she would seek out a room at the local YWCA instead of staying at a good (and expensive) hotel.

Visiting our family in our childhood, she would take us children off to nearby woods to play by a little stream. She tried to inspire us with her love of nature, identifying the birds we saw and heard, finding edible mushrooms, having us watch spiders spin their webs. We remained skittish with creepy, crawly things, but we did not gloatingly squash them in her presence.

I never became a professional bird watcher, but no home of mine — except when it was a city apartment — has ever been without some sort of bird feeding and watering equipment. It gives one such a bountiful feeling on hot days to fill a shallow dish with cool water, and watch a mockingbird steal in for a long drink, or a robin splash and shake and splash again!

Perhaps it was our early love affair with the baby robin, *Dixie*, but I have a special affection for robins. They are too busy living to worry and fuss. They go devotedly and enthusiastically about the business of raising their families, but take no nonsense from demanding fledglings. Their liquid, throaty song at dawn and dusk proclaims fulfillment. I don't even mind being waked by it at 5 A.M.! I can drift back to drowsiness, knowing the sun rises, as well as sets, and that — no matter the newspaper headlines — spring will continue to return to the land and to our hearts.

As children in those days, we were not privy to our parents' opinions about other adults. Adults, then, maintained a solid front against the curious, impertinent attempts of children to learn what goes on between grown-ups. I suspect some resentment toward Auntie Anna on Mother's part — perhaps the unacknowledged envy of a woman with family responsibilities toward the woman without them?

Auntie Anna's writing case accompanied her wherever she went. If she must wait for an appointment or train, she would sit, scribbling letters to friends all over the country — the world — because wherever she went, she added more friends to the host of those with whom she kept in touch.

She never forgot family birthdays, but she was not one to shop. For us children, there would always be a small, pretty card, with a check for one dollar enclosed. Money is so important to so many people. In her life, it was just a necessary nuisance.

Birthdays reassured us that we were always loved and wanted. Carefully wrapped presents lay beside our breakfast plates. Not the mind-boggling stacks of gifts children nowadays receive, but one or two things we had most longed for.

On our birthdays, we could also choose what we wanted for dinner. Betty once confused everybody by asking for "little fishes." It was finally determined she meant sardines!

And for ten years, in faraway Elmira, Grandma Pratt baked and decorated angel food birthday cakes, sending them to us — in those pre-Parcel Post days — by American Express.

Our parents were regular churchgoers, as were most conscientious middle-class parents of their day. However, neither of them spent much time serving on committees. They thought it more important to do things with their children.

Father had little patience with the Sunday Schools of that day. He disapproved of the emphasis on sin and punishment, and the more recent "clap-hands-Jesus-loves-me" pap. He believed in the Bible as the Word of God and the magnificent interpretation of man's aspirations and destiny. He did not want us growing up Bible illiterates.

Instead of sending us off to Sunday School, while he read the papers or slept, he taught us himself, every Sunday evening of childhood, all of us sitting in our living room after an early supper.

We learned something of the background of the Old and New Testaments. We read the Bible stories, and were helped to a child's understanding of their lessons. Then we sang hymns, Mother at the piano. And we did a lot of memorizing of Bible verses and Psalms.

Memorizing is frowned on today. As a substitute for thought, analysis, logic, it should be. But we missed so much when we quit learning good poetry and inspiring prose! Children memorize so easily — and it *lasts*. Most of us recall childhood jingles. The Psalms that I learned in our home Sunday School so many years ago still bring me calm and comfort in times of strain and stress.

The same is true of the poetry I had to memorize in school. When the wait in the doctor's office drags on, and the copies of *Time* on his magazine table are six months old, sanity can be sustained by silently running through the 19th century poems I once had to learn — and came later to love.

A niece once asked — "How were holidays celebrated when you were young?"

I had to stop and think — Haven't there always been Thanksgivings and Christmases?

Yes, but Halloween was not the big deal it now is. I don't remember trick-or-treating. Perhaps our parents did not approve of our ringing doorbells and holding up bags for candy.

The Fourth of July, however — in New England — was both noisy and glorious! That was *America's birthday* — to be celebrated with loud enthusiasm. We were not allowed firecrackers like other children, but there was always a Fourth of July parade to watch, and we usually ate fresh salmon and the first new garden peas for dinner.

Sometimes there would be a picnic supper on our lawn, and when it got dark — instead of being sent to bed — we could race about with "sparklers." Sometimes Father set off (with caution and a pail of water handy) a small supply of rockets and pinwheels. The awe and wonder of those explosions of dazzling light against a dark sky was comparable to that engendered 80 years later by reading Carl Sagan's *Cosmos*.

Two months earlier was May Day.

A pale New England sun would be promising later warmth, so mothers had quit hollering — "Come back now! You forgot your coat!"

For a week we would have been decorating old candy boxes with fringes of tissue paper, filling them with homemade fudge, and — at the last minute — sticking in one or two early, wilted daffodils or dandelions. The first day of May we tore around the neighborhood, hanging them on the doorknobs of our little friends' homes. And then — excitement and delight! — arriving breathless back home to find May baskets hanging from *our* front door knob!

We did not carry flowers to the cemetery on Memorial Day, which was then known as "Decoration Day": our graves were in far-away Amherst or Elmira. But neither did we go on bargain-hunting binges. We stood on the sidewalk for the Decoration Day parade, which featured "our boys in blue" — old men with tired feet and bent shoulders — some in horse-drawn carriages. We applauded vigorously but respectfully.

There were always special school observances, when some boy would recite Lincoln's Gettysburg Address. Once I had to memorize Thomas Bailey Aldrich's *Spring in New England*. Father spent several evenings coaching me, so I probably performed quite well, and was asked to repeat it at the town celebration in the Square. To my lasting disappointment, Father and Mother agreed between themselves that I was much too young to stand up on the platform with the town fathers.

On Confederate Memorial Day in June in Moorefield, C.B. and other barefoot boys in knee pants and clean white shirts, would climb the steep, winding road to the cemetery carrying long ropes of cedar on their shoulders — ropes to be wound around the graves of the Men in Gray, which circled the tall Confederate War Memorial. His later memory of it all was of the itching from prickly cedar needles scratching sweaty little necks!

It is the same Memorial Day now. At the end of the first World War, C.B.'s dad wrote a brief, eloquent letter to the Town Council, pointing out that the men in gray and the khaki-clad boys, who never returned from France, had all died for their country, and should be honored together. I once saw that letter, but I do not know what became of it.

Christmas meant hanging our long black stockings from the fireplace mantle, tiptoeing downstairs at daylight to retrieve them; then crawling back under the covers in under-heated bedrooms, to push small hands into their dark depths, and haul forth a handful of hard candy, a glowing orange.

About dark the living room door would be opened to the marvel of the lighted Christmas tree — and Santa Claus.

Later — the inevitable question — ''Was it *really* Santa?... Or could it have been Papa?''

But no trauma accompanied this discovery. It simply reenforced our understanding that good things happened because we were — Our Family!

Chapter 11

A West Virginia Thanksgiving

Over the river and through the woods
To Grandmother's house we go.
The horse knows the way to carry the sleigh
O'er the white and drifting snow.

Every small New Englander used to know Lydia M. Child's Thanksgiving poem. And when we were *very* young, we had known what it was like to ride behind a great, steaming horse, in a cozy, old-time sleigh.

Such constituted a faint but exhilerating memory of sparkling, cold air, snuggly warm lap robes, and the squeak of runner on hard-packed snow. We used to ask:

"Will we have a sleigh ride this year?"

But the time came when even children knew that sleigh runners would drag in the tracks left by automobile tires.

Our grandmothers' homes were too distant for Thanksgiving dinners in those days, when flying was unknown and driving even a hundred miles impossible, since everybody had to go back to work on Friday and Saturday.

Nor did the telephone provide "togetherness." Long distance calls, difficult to "put through," were for births and deaths, not casual greetings or hour-long conversations.

Thanksgiving today is a brief interval of feasting and football sandwiched in between the trick-or-treat fantastics of Halloween, and the annual orgy of Christmas giving.

The New England Thanksgiving of my childhood ranked along with Christmas in importance. It might be a day gloriously to stuff ourselves, but it was also a day to remember our Pilgrim heritage and be grateful for creature comforts and family ties. If it was impossible to join grandparents for the day, it was important to include — if possible — any who might be alone on that family-oriented occasion.

99

In my early years in the Mountain State, I learned that the fourth Thursday in November was deer season first, Thanksgiving day second. In Hardy County, at least, all males were off before daylight, heading for the hills, their deer rifles in the trunks of their cars. In Massachusetts, Father's carving of the turkey had been a ritual of deftness and mouth-watering anticipation. In West Virginia, the women were more likely to cut up the turkey in the kitchen, while the men cleaned up after the hunt.

But there was one West Virginia Thanksgiving that no one who lived in Moorefield will ever forget. It was what Giving Thanks is all about.

November 4, 1985 was the fifth day of downpour in our mountains — a storm spawned by Hurricane Juan — which dumped 19 inches of rain on the headwaters of the Potomac in the hills south of us.

November 4, 1985. . . Days of wet weather frustration have become an hour of high-water apprehension as Mayor Larry Kuykendall drives back and forth across the river to discuss flood warnings with radio station WELD — "Your country music station" — on the hill west of town. On his last trip over, he leaves his police scanner there with owner-operator, Willard Earle. Turning off the bridge, as he heads back toward town, he suddenly realizes his truck is close to floating.

Trying to think what to do next, he first opens the dog pound and carries some young pups to the safety of the Town Shed. He knows of two pregnant women, almost ready to deliver. Should he try to do something about them?

WELD finally utters the "F" word — FLOOD! — and urges those who may be endangered by high water to take immediate refuge in the grade school. . . But the school has been built since "the last big flood" — 1949 — and it is on the flood plain!

The mayor has also thought of drinking-water, and the town tanks on the hill east are full with over a million gallons. But logs from the hills and mills, riding the coming wild crest, will smash the fire hydrants and loose every drop.

Disaster is something we watch on TV, sitting comfortably in a warm room, like Lena Harrison, 80, among her antiques, watching the storm news on the screen and wondering about the roaring noise outside. Volunteer firemen had to guide her out through rushing, waist-deep water, along a rope tied to the giant road grader, serving as a rescue vehicle, after — at her request — rolling up her Oriental rugs and laying them on tables.

I had been living for five years in a little house near the center of town. But — watching the rain that afternoon, listening to the radio — I remember 1949, run water in the tub and fill the refrigerator with jars of drinking water. I go to bed in warm shirt and slacks, with boots and purse close by. Surprising myself, I fall soundly asleep.

At 2 A.M. my neighbor, Dr. Maxwell's finger bears down on my doorbell.

"I can't believe it will reach *us*," he says, "but the order has come to evacuate town, and I'm not going to argue."

A few did. Robin Hoard futilely urged her parents to flee their mobile home. They were swept to their deaths when it broke apart. She clung all night to a gas station pump, with her daughter tied to her, till daylight brought a rescue helicopter. Gray-haired Nettie and Sara Brooks had been told their grandfather had built their home above any high-water mark. They were clinging together, praying together atop their upstairs four-poster, when the rising waters finally halted at their knees.

A line of car lights winds up Cemetery Hill (as the little boys had, long ago, with their cedar swags) and families huddle together in the cold near the century-old gravestones. Those sheltering in the schools are evacuated a second, frightening time to the Brethren Church on somewhat higher ground. Lucky ones — like me — share a room or sofa in homes of relatives or friends above the floor of the valley.

At daylight, I make my way back downhill, where wet and exhausted firemen are telling stopped cars what we are already seeing for ourselves: not all of us can go home.

Six hours before — taking a last look at the cherished family heirlooms, as I locked the door — I'd firmly reminded myself —

"Remember — they're only *things*!"

But beloved things! Handled not only by me but by my parents and grandparents. Turning the key again, after daylight, seeing it all dry and undisturbed — the relief is almost as overwhelming as the sight of the flooded town had been.

A heavy quiet hangs over my immediate neighborhood. A few are walking gingerly about, eyeing backyards below, where strange objects eddy in muddy water. We speak softly, as if greeting each other in a funeral parlor. A block downhill, Moorefield's one stoplight changes steadily from red to green and red again above five or six feet of swift, dark water.

No one has yet heard of desperate rescues and vain attempts, of bridges gone and trailers swept onto the highways. Telephones are out. Nobody knows anything more than what he can see for himself — that much of the town is under water. Nobody, one realizes, in the state or nation, knows what has happened to the "Poultry Capital of West Virginia." When the first call finally gets through, late in the day, the mayor says —

"Tell them to get us drinking water!"

For five days after that, all of us — men and women, young and old — carry pails and bottles to and from the tank trucks that, by the next afternoon, are parked in front of the Town Hall. National Guardsmen, suddenly seen patrolling the town, politely help old ladies like myself, who find it not that easy — at age 86 — to carry two pails of water two blocks!

WELD has gone off the air shortly after 2 A.M. with the phone dead and the power out. But Willard, his wife, and their three-year-old daughter are stuck there, because the bridge approach from town has washed out. They spend three days and nights at the station, with neighbors from the surrounding high ground coming in to baby-sit and bring milk and sandwiches.

But they have the mayor's police scanner, and that morning of November 5, they are contacted by the police radio.

"It was strictly not legal," the mayor later explained, "but it was all we could do. Nobody's hassled us."

Thus, those in the town office could telephone the railroad office, which had a radio, and those there could radio WELD. Then Willard would broadcast the messages handed him by his wife, who was writing them down as they came in over this Rube Goldberg setup.

"Goldie Moran, please let your family know where you are... Wayne Crites, please notify family and friends... Gayle — we didn't catch the last name — Gary is in town and OK and trying to get home... Jim Flinn, please let your family know" — and again, later — "Does anybody know anything about Jim Flinn?"

Flinn was dead of a heart attack.

"Need food for 200 people at Rig. Deliver to Community Center. Food that requires no cooking..."

The morning after the flood finds a house trailer lodged across North Main St. in Moorefield.

Later, ham operators pushed in over the debris-strewn roads, from Winchester, Virginia, and Cumberland, Maryland, widening and maintaining communications.

The West Virginia mountaineer has made "hillbilly" a proud term. From the early days, he has helped himself and his neighbors. Before the Salvation Army got there with 3,000 peanut butter sandwiches; before the competent, friendly Red Cross girls; before even the Mennonite disaster-trained workers with their cleanup equipment and their own sandwiches; and well before the FEMA staffers, with their forms and files and briefcases, Moorefield organized itself.

"We'd done so much for so long with so little" said the mayor, "we thus attempted the impossible with nothing . . . I read that somewhere. But that's the way we managed."

Owners of undamaged homes offered beds to the homeless. Food, clothing and cleaning supplies, being trucked in, were dispensed from the Presbyterian Church parking lot, floodwaters having damaged the church's interior. The Brethren Church averaged 900 free meals a day for two weeks.

Teachers joined janitors in shoveling mud out of classrooms, dragging desks outside to hose them down. Library patrons sloshed in to pull hundreds of damaged books, scrub the shelves and stack equipment, so that professional cleaners could later pump 400 gallons of muddy water out of the almost-new carpet. Old ladies hunched over crowded tables in the Town Office, writing out passes for those leaving or entering town through the National Guard lines.

Ernie Combs, local trash collector, donated a week's free time, gas and labor on the part of himself and his crew, to clear debris from yards and streets. He moved 1,600 truckloads. In spite of mud in the machinery, the *Moorefield Examiner* put out a four-page flood edition.

Farmers buried dozens of dead cattle. Their wives threw out hundreds of quarts of home-canned beans and tomatoes, which had stood under water in flooded cellars, remembering — as they worked — the heat and weariness of summer canning, and worrying over winter food shortages to come. Two live cows were pulled out of John Sherman's swimming pool. A dump truck, parked near the center of town, bore the sign — "Please put small, dead animals here." The bank telephoned us to come get our safety deposit boxes, empty out the muddy water and spread the contents to dry out on beds and tables at home.

At first we watched a couple of helicopters moving up- and downstream, in search of bodies or survivors. Most of the former were found days later by search parties on foot, struggling through acres of downed trees and trash, cemented with mud.

But after a few days, nobody gawked upward any more, as the whirlybirds landed and lifted off, ferrying food and tools, and delivering chicken feed to remote poultry houses on the hillsides. And, of course, dropping off congressmen, senators, the governor, a general, a female FEMA director, and their aides, assistants, press officers and photographers.

A milking machine, urgently needed 40 miles upstream, waits to be loaded, its delivery vehicle circling impatiently above, while the VIP transportation idles on the pad, waiting for the politicians and the military to stop talking and head back to Charleston, West Virginia or Washington, DC.

Later, the mud was the worst thing. It had to be shoveled, shoveled again, scraped, sopped, mopped, before streets and floors were halfway clean. It turned metal green; it was slick as butter. Only the young and agile dared cross the streets.

When Thanksgiving was next week, we knew we were going to make it. As food continued to pour in, including holiday turkeys, it was announced that a free Thanksgiving dinner would be served to the entire town. Any and all would be welcome. This was not only to insure that no gift turkeys spoiled or families in need were forgotten, but our sense of kinship now went beyond family and friends and included everyone who'd shared the experience of what was now being called the 500-year-flood.

Housewives with working stoves roasted the gift turkeys in their ovens. Potatoes, trucked in by farmers from Ohio and Pennsylvania, were peeled, cooked and mashed by thankful women whose own homes had been spared. Steve Wilson, restaurant proprietor, who — with the town's ministers and leaders — had planned this affair, baked two thousand rolls.

Thanksgiving dinner was served from Noon to 3 P.M. at four different locations — the Methodist and Brethren churches, which had both escaped flood damage, the Senior Citizens' Center (formerly the old library building), and the Old Stone Tavern restaurant, where efforts were coordinated. Young people carried the platters of turkey and dressing, the bowls of beans or gravy or slaw between the centers. Mothers and daughters filled plates, waited on tables.

From out-of-state deer hunters (who left generous donations for their dinners) to some who would otherwise have gone hungry that holiday, it was a traditional family feast — a Thanksgiving dinner that will never be forgotten by those who planned it, cooked it or ate it.

To this New Englander, with her long tradition of old-time Thanksgivings, it was probably the most thankful one since that which took place in the Massachusetts Bay Colony nearly 400 years ago!

Our Christmas lights went up in town a week later. They had never swung so proudly. Homes and stores hung makeshift decorations; the old "boughten" ones were in sodden boxes, carted to the town dump. A community church cantata was hastily rehearsed and sung two nights to capacity audiences in the Brethren Church.

Volunteers, trudging the muddy streets in the cold (to be sure all homes had been visited, all those in need, identified and informed of all available aid resources), were met with such words as:

"Don't bother about us! We're lucky — we've still got our home. We'll make it back! Folks who've lost their houses or their kin — they're the ones you need to see — not us."

In the cities, that December, elaborate lights sparkled, opulent store windows glowed, heedless crowds flowed in and out of cars, stores, offices. In our West Virginia hills, the corn was flat, the farm-lands trashed, the stores empty of supplies, the homes (many of them) damaged and without gifts — or even necessities.

But we had seen the spirit of Thanksgiving and Christmas in the hearts and hands of so many kind, generous, anonymous Americans, who had flown or driven to our aid, with milk and mops and money, with sheets and shirts and winter underwear, and the will to work alongside us in the muddy soil of salvage.

A rough winter for many was ahead. But we knew that spring would one day return, with gardens green again, and the dogwood misting the hills.

Chapter 12

Some "Firsts"

My father bought me my first cocktail.

This, no doubt, will shock some good, church-going friends. But — seventy-odd years later — I remember it with gratitude.

He had taken me to dinner at a nice New York restaurant. It might have been while I was still in college, although trips to New York, in those days, were rare for Vassar undergraduates, who must have parents' written permission; must sign out, sign in — unbelievable procedures to today's students, who seem to spend as much time off campus as *in* college! More likely, it was in my early newspaper days.

I don't remember what he ordered, but it was cool and smooth, and he touched his glass to mine.

"I want you to know that a drink should be enjoyed with family or friends, and at a meal. Not gulped down guiltily, or taken under pressure from a crowd. I think — if you know this is the way it should be done — neither of us will have to worry about the drinking problem."

Neither of us ever had reason to.

Father kept a little whiskey in the house. He and Mother may occasionally have served wine at a dinner party. In their circle of friends — before Prohibition — there was little to no drinking. It would never have occurred to me then that people I *knew* would drink too much at a social gathering... How long ago that was!

Living and working in New York in the early years of Prohibition was something else. I shared a Greenwich Village apartment (after that first rooming house) with another college girl whom I had met there. We were soon introduced to speakeasies and "bathtub gin." We went to our share of dark restaurants, where we were inspected through a peephole, before the door was slowly and silently opened. There was that thrill of illicit excitement, but I was not completely besotted by it. My upbringing had made me somewhat contemptuous of what — in my childhood — would have been referred to as "goings-on."

Having made the acquaintance of bootleg liquor in New York, I was introduced to moonshining in West Virginia.

On an early visit there, C.B. and I were invited to see a moonshine still in operation. In spite of occasional speakeasies, the Boston blond was basically law-abiding — and always timid. I was scared at the thought of this expedition and, naturally, afraid to let it be known I had qualms.

Two or three cars of young people drove several miles out of town and turned off on a farm lane past a dark house. Car lights were doused as soon as we left the highway. In the thick dark, we drove a mile or so up a lane and then turned into an open field. At some point, the cars stopped, engines were shut off. We got out and one set of headlights was turned on and off in an obviously prearranged signal.

I did not see any return signal, but — after a minute or two — we were told it was OK to proceed. Following the others, I stumbled through a meadow, up a dark and rocky hillside, until I suddenly glimpsed firelight ahead. We emerged into a rocky hollow, where a still was running full blast, tended by a slight young man wearing a gun on each hip. He boasted proudly to the men in our group that he could shoot equally well with left or right hand.

The quart jar, into which a clear liquid was dropping from a copper coil, started to overflow, and somebody picked it up and handed it around. It was clear — like water. But it *didn't taste like water!*

Taking a cautious sip, I suddenly remembered what — in my reading of frontier days — Indians had called the white man's whiskey — "firewater"! I thought — "I don't dare swallow — I'll choke to death!" I tried to smack my dry lips, murmured something appreciative, and quickly passed the jar to the girl next to me.

The liquor tasted, the process explained for the benefit of "city folks," the amenities concluded, we moved back down the hillside, coming suddenly upon the cars in the heavy darkness. Again without lights, we drove through the meadow, and back down the narrow lane, until the highway came in sight. When the headlights blazed again, I found myself suddenly relieved and relaxed.

C.B. was not the hard-drinking newspaperman of fiction and drama. He could nurse a glass all evening, listen appreciatively to others and tell a better story himself. He was always part of the group, yet always his own man; unlike many of us who seem subtley to change, as we move from one group to another. He treated all men with equal courtesy, and all women with courtliness — but never condescension, granting them — unspokenly — equal ability and intellect. Perhaps that is why he was a close and trusted friend of Amelia Earhart's. . . But that comes later.

When *The New York World* realized that a member of its city staff was a flyer, C.B. was assigned to cover aviation events, and later given the title of aviation editor, one he held from 1923 to 1954, with *The World*, the *World-Telegram* and the *New York Herald-Tribune*. His first such assignment was the return of the Army's Round-the-World Flyers. They had left Seattle in April of 1924, and returned to the American continent in September. *The World* sent him to Pictou, Nova Scotia to meet them on their return.

It was a longer wait than expected, and *World* editor Swope, in the comfort of his New York inner sanctum, fired off several telegrams about how the story should be covered — not all of them pertinent to the situation as it existed in that cold, distant, isolated spot. C.B. eventually sent back one of his own, which simply said:

"This is Murray Bay, not Murray Hill."

When Lindbergh took off for Paris in 1927 from Roosevelt Field, C.B. and "Deac" Lyman of the *New York Times* were hunkered down behind a steamroller, which had been used to smooth the runway, and then left at the end of the field just where it dropped off slightly. This was the point where C.B. knew Lindbergh must be airborne or crash. His plane cleared them and the steamroller by about ten feet. And the rest is history.

C.B. kept his commission in the Air Corps Reserve, so that he could fly whenever possible, including his annual two weeks' active duty tour every summer. Occasionally, friends in the industry (they were many) loaned him a plane. Thus, on one occasion, we were able to make a trip together.

His dad had recently remarried, and was living on his wife's Kansas farm. C.B. thought we might fly out there and visit them.

The plane was an Aero-Marine Klemm, a low-wing monoplane, with a 40-horsepower engine, which did not make much speed against prevailing west winds. We would look down from a height of some 1,500 feet and see the few cars on the two-lane highways traveling faster than we!

The plane's design also meant that we were not only exposed to the direct rays of the sun, but to additional reflected glare from the wings. We were badly sunburned. This was long before suntans were fashionable and tanning creams and lotions available. Cold cream dissolved in greasy rivulets. Smearing ourselves with theatrical greasepaint saved the day and our skins.

Our only instrument was a compass, and our only navigation aid was a set of old automobile maps, by which we followed the rail lines west. Sometimes the tracks diverged, and we would have to guess which one to follow. If the guess was correct, the next town would show up off the wing tips, where the maps said it was. When we followed the wrong tracks, C.B. would fly low over the next railroad station, banking the plane, so I could read the station name.

Once I identified the small shack in an empty expanse of sandy waste, as Menonly. C.B. checked the map; then his shoulders shook with laughter. I had read the sign on the restroom door!

The second or third day, making poor time against headwinds, we were short of our destination. The sun ahead was perilously close to setting. I sensed his concern and became nervous. Fortunately, I couldn't communicate from back seat to front, without touching him on the shoulder, and I had sense enough to know I had nothing to communicate except anxiety — and he already had enough of that.

Finally he saw what looked to be a racecourse surrounded by trees. Circling low, he decided it was a possible landing spot, side-slipped neatly in — and the plane rolled to a stop.

As always, in those early days of flying, if a plane was seen coming in for a landing, two or three cars immediately showed up alongside the field, hoping (doubtless) to witness a crash! The occupant of one such provided us a ride into town and a stop at the one hotel.

The trees encircling the racetrack were tall, and the next morning C.B. realized it would not be easy to take off and clear them with a passenger and baggage aboard.

There was nothing for it, but for me to take a bus and the baggage to the next city, which happened to be Terre Haute, Indiana, while he tried to lift the Klemm up and out over the treetops.

He put me on the bus, with our one suitcase in the rack above, and the plane's spare tire and tools in my lap. The bus was full, and I couldn't get a window seat. So I sat quietly by the aisle, trying to haul my mind back from what would happen if the Klemm didn't clear the trees.

He had said — "I'll pick up the bus on the highway, fly down where you can see me and waggle the wings."

The flat countryside rolled by. I sat and waited.

Then the woman next to me by the window looked up and said — "Oh! There's an airplane!"

I pushed the spare tire to the floor, leaned across her and looked up and out. The plane's wings were waggling! It was the Klemm!

The road maps took us to Kansas, and the town nearest the farm. His dad had written it was four or five miles from a white church with a high steeple. We could find no such landmark.

C.B. picked an open field near a farmhouse, and brought the plane in for a landing. A white-haired, overalled farmer strode across the meadow. C.B. climbed out and asked if he happened to know the location of the Curran farm.

You might have thought it commonplace for an airplane to drop out of the sky to ask directions. Without seeming the least surprised, the old man explained where we were and what to look for. We thanked him and took off again.

The church's "high steeple" proved to be a two-story block, and once we realized that, we had no trouble locating the small farmhouse and landing again in a nearby pasture.

This was my first meeting with Miss Annie.

The farmhouse was small, the furnishings sparse and simple, but there was within an air of peace and plenty. Out back was a very clean privy, and in the kitchen, a neat iron pump on a white painted iron sink. Both were totally dry.

We were seeing firsthand the terrible drought of the 1930s. Never before had I known what it meant to be *without water*! I was shocked out of my city complacency to see the care — yes, the *reverence* — with which water was handled — doled out — saved. The house well was long dry. Miss Annie had to drive her old Model T Ford some 4-5 miles to a well in a distant slough, where water was hauled up in a heavy bucket, emptied carefully into a couple of five-gallon milk cans — taking care not to spill a single drop. Then she drove the Ford home, and Dad helped her unload the cans.

We dipped water from the cans into a small pitcher, emptied a little into a small washpan, bathed, and poured the dirty water into a pail under the sink, whence it would be carried to the barnyard for the cows and chickens.

When you follow that routine for a few days, you can never again let a faucet run carelessly!

Droughts come and go. The oceans are forever. Reading news headlines of Pan-American's bankruptcy, I remembered the proud "Clipper Ships" on which C.B. made so many "first" passenger flights across the then uncharted reaches of the world's oceans.

Today we have left behind the deserts and the oceans to rocket into outer space. I read history and pre-history, where advances occurred over ages. And I, personally, am recalling the 20th century, when travel went from ten miles an hour to hundreds of miles a minute!

Yesterday's pioneers of the airways — Lindbergh, Chamberlin, Bernt Balchen, Casey Jones, and many others — talked to C.B., not as to a reporter, but as to one who also knew the feel of the stick in the hands, and the lift of air beneath the wings. They spoke the same language, and it was not that of coin and commerce, but of the human spirit pitted against the elements and the fates.

Lindburgh was notorious for his dislike of the press. But he trusted two newspapermen — C.B. and "Deac" Lyman. Amelia Earhart asked C.B.'s advice on many occasions and about many of her flights. From the last one — when she chose to ignore it — she did not return.

Voice radio was a new development in 1937, and was installed in her Lockheed Electra in preparation for her round-the-world flight. Before taking off from Miami, she told C.B. she had decided to dispense with her wireless equipment, because it added too much weight.

"And, anyway, I'm not very good at Morse Code," were her concluding words to him on the subject.

He had demurred at this. In the event of a forced landing, ships at sea would have been able to get a definite fix on her location, when she held down the key on the transmitter. But she returned to the weight argument, and was certain she could remain in touch — through voice communication — with the U.S. Navy vessels, which would be listening for her.

Again — the rest is history.

Amelia Earhart with C.B. Allen just before her final take-off.

C.B. had little patience with all the spy and secret mission theories, which, for a time, circulated widely. He felt that what undoubtedly happened was what Mary S. Lovell wrote in her recent Earhart biography, *The Sound of Wings:*

"All the documented facts point to a ditching off Howland Island, which neither flier survived."

When Claire Booth Luce was editor of *Vanity Fair* magazine, she asked C.B. to write a series of articles on learning to fly. At her request, he rented a small plane at Roosevelt Field and took her up, so she could feel for herself what it was like to fly like this. At some point, the engine conked out, and he was forced to make a "dead-stick" landing.

It was a beautiful day, and she had obviously been enjoying the scenery and the flight.

"But why are we landing here, Mr. Allen?" she asked, after they had rolled to a stop.

"Lady, you've had your first forced landing," he told her.

It did not, however, destroy her enthusiasm for flying, nor her confidence in him as a pilot, for, of the series he wrote, the magazine said:

"Mr. C.B. Allen himself learned to fly in the United States Army during the world war, and has been a gentleman of the air ever since. He holds a Transport Pilot's license, and a Captain's commission in the Air Corps Reserve. Aviation editor of the *World-Telegram*, he is one of the few newspapermen who is also an active flyer. He won the Sportsmen Pilot's cup at the National Air Races in Chicago in 1930, taking 'time out' from the press box to do so. A year ago he flew Lindbergh's Curtis Falcon across the continent to cover the Air Corps maneuvers at Mather Field. He was the first passenger (1927) to go through with the mail in continuous flight from New York to San Francisco. He toured Europe with Clarence D. Chamberlin and was co-author of his *Record Flights*. He covered the Army Air Corps 'big parade' over New York this year by radio-telegram into the *World-Telegram*'s office, from a plane which paced the 'raiders' down the Hudson. And that, ladies and gentlemen, is flying."

Two or three times I was able to accompany C.B. to the National Air Races in Cleveland and Chicago, and had the fun of sitting in the press box and being passably useful checking laps during the races.

I could understand how he felt about flying, but try as I might, I could not share his feelings. Whenever I could go with him — which wasn't that often in those early days, when we could afford no extra expense — I went gladly. But I was always apprehensive. I hated that. I didn't want to be afraid — but I couldn't seem to help it.

When — on leave from the *New York Herald-Tribune* — he worked in Washington with the Civil Aeronautics Authority, and later as the third member of the first independent Air Safety Board, we lived in nearby Virginia, and I took flying lessons, hoping this would help. They gave me a sense of what it was like to be free of the earth — to ride the sky as one drives the highways — with a feeling of release and exhileration. Perhaps I could sometime have fallen in love with it, as I had with him.

I did — eventually — solo. And C.B. was proud and pleased for me, for he knew it had not been easy. It was a part of his world he was willing to share. But I could not get past the threshhold.

Chapter 13

Values

"Family values" — in this present day — is a phrase seen and heard daily in the press and on the lips of politicians. It wasn't one our parents used, but the concept was clearly understood by their children.

We understood our parents expected us to do well in school, and thus homework was to be tackled right after dinner in the quiet solitude of our own rooms.

But except for school and homework, our time was not structured. We were not driven from tennis lessons to dancing class to soccer games to choir practice. We were expected to entertain ourselves.

Of course we were often bored and dissatisfied — as are most children, even when they're constantly being chauffeured from here to there. We would storm into the house, fling ourselves down —

"But Mother! There's nothing to DO!"

Her answers depended on the seasons, and probably her own frustrations.

"You could have a tea party for your dolls — and fix lemonade . . . Why don't you get your sled and go coasting? . . . Worse — "Your closet is a mess. Now's a good time to straighten it up." Which of course, sent us back out to play in the yard.

Organized sports, I'm happy to remember, did not happen until our secondary school days. We played outdoors whenever the weather permitted, which meant (New England weather being what it always has been) that only downpours or blizzards kept us in.

I don't particularly remember the games. They involved a lot of running, jumping up and down and yelling. The yelling was our own, excited and happy. There were no partisan parents, nor professional coaches to yell at an eight-year-old for missing a good shot.

Our parents did not spend much money or thought on entertainment for us or for themselves. Commercial entertainments were not aimed at children in those early days of the twentieth century. Theme parks and fantasy worlds, with their stiff admission fees, and infinite ploys to extract cash after one is inside, had not yet been built. In Wellesley Hills, it was a rare treat to visit a small, nearby amusement park, where the big excitement was deciding whether to ride the horse, the giraffe or the lion on the one merry-go-round.

A twenty-minute trolley ride to Sunderland was our Amherst treat. We would scramble up on the bench right behind the motorman, if others did not already occupy this desirable spot. There, the wind would blow in our faces and we could watch his right hand on the control bar, and his left foot hitting the bell to warn of starts and stops. The gentle rural countryside rolled past in the warm summer sun — neat farmhouses, tobacco fields, cows — maybe a collie to dash out and bark at us! Almost a half hour of new sights for the price of a nickle!

At the Sunderland end of the line, we would slide off, walk about a bit, watch closely the switching of the trolley for the return trip, and climb back on. Half a day's drive in a car could not have been more satisfying.

Vacation trips were rare in that era of the five-and-a-half-day work-week. Whether Father managed his own business (which he too often tried) or was employed by others, he found tremendous satisfaction in his work, spending long hours in office or laboratory. I know that Mother, brought up in an academic household, where long summer vacations — even occasional trips to Europe — were the norm, was upset by this, and tried — without success — to get him to take more time off.

We made one disastrous trip to Block Island. We were all, except Father, so seasick on the rough trip across the sound that, by the time we had spent two days in the hotel recovering, it was time to return home.

Eating out was also a rare treat in that pre-Fast Food era. We would not have dared to fuss and fidget when food was long in coming, but developed our own way to cope by pretending to play a close chess game, moving the cutlery with intense concentration, "jumping" a salt-cellar over a spoon with a silent flourish. We never created any disturbance, but Mother would sometimes be embarrassed to see other diners closely watching our moves.

Even a drugstore sundae was not commonplace. One I have remembered for eighty years!

Sundaes were then ten cents. The Amherst drugstore sold an "ice cream card," entitling the happy owner to twelve sundaes for one dollar. Every time it was used, the soda clerk punched the numbered space.

One day, in our customary childhood rambles about town, we found, by the roadside, an ice cream card with *one punch* left on it. We stared at it, unable to believe our luck.

Then we raced back to the drugstore, scrambled up on three stools and ordered a vanilla-ice-cream-with-chocolate-sauce-and-nuts-and-whipped-cream-and-a-cherry sundae. And *three spoons!*

We took careful turns — we had been brought up always to be fair and share. But I don't remember who got the cherry.

While activities were not organized, music lessons were offered, and we walked once a week to the music teacher's home, and back. I kept on for several enjoyable years, but the other two were bored and begged off. Father was not musical, C.B. even less so, but years after my childhood lessons had ended, he was the one to give me the means to lifetime music.

My father loved to buy and give gifts. So it was an early disappointment that C.B. — like many men — didn't seem to think of it. Many men do not realize wives yearn for an appropriate gift as proof they are cherished. I had never known "many men." But I finally grew to understand that love needs no penny proof. When C.B. realized how much I'd enjoyed the loan of a piano, while its owner was in Europe, he asked a professional pianist to help him buy the best piano he could afford — that would fit in our living room.

Our parents didn't talk a lot about money.

I'm sure the subject existed importantly in the background of their thinking. They would often have wondered — will there be enough for the children's education, their highest priority? And Father — always extravagant where his family was concerned — must often have wondered whether he could pay his bills.

But so much else occupied his thinking — inventions he was working on, discoveries he hoped to make, philosophies that challenged his concepts — *making money* was never all that important. He seemed to assume it would inevitably follow his efforts.

But like many others in the years of the Great Depression, my father went bankrupt. He must previously have had some business success, as a result of his processes and patents, for he had had built for himself a new laboratory building, of which he was very proud.

The laboratory, and the home in which I had grown up and married, were both sold to satisfy his creditors, and he and Mother lived for a while until his death, in a rented Boston apartment. He used to work his chemical experiments in the small kitchen. His creditors could seize his possessions; his creative mind was beyond their reach.

It was then, when his dreams were dissolving, his heart failing, that he once said to me —

"Learn to *want* what you already *have!*"

Others would have used the more passive and pious — "Be thankful for what you've got." It was the strength of his drive that made him say "want." He realized he craved achievement and acclaim, but he knew what his family meant to him.

One thing he always had was our mother's fierce loyalty. She might wonder at his misplaced enthusiasms, regret his mistakes. But in all the years of their marriage, I never heard her complain or wish things were different.

Her life, when we were small, was made up of housework and child care — which many women today think they must escape. Few women of her day had, or expected to have "careers." They were housewives, an honorable designation, attained through marriage.

Hers was a marriage of love, and the children were welcomed. Thus love was the foundation of her life — passionate love, family love, love of order and beauty in her home.

I know that it is from her that I inherit my delight in my own home. If I could never again touch the old mahogany, handle the antique silver, I should indeed be bereft.

I cannot but believe this is the way she felt. Otherwise, I would not know it so certainly in my hands as well as my heart. And thus know that her life as "just a housewife" was still one of joy and creativity.

When our father died, it never occurred to her to turn back to her painting. That belonged — like the old dance-cards — to a youth long gone. Loneliness engulfed her, but her children's homes offered her no refuge.

My father, William Beach Pratt (about 1920).

From some forgotten well of independence, she drew on her own resources, and made beautifully hand knit things for a local craft shop. And then, on her own — asking no one's advice, and never having done anything like this in all her seventy and more years — she found herself a job as a comparison shopper for a Boston department store.

Once, without her understanding of the situation, she was asked to have some dealings with a clerk suspected of stealing. When her testimony was later sought, her New England sense of what was just and honorable, took her straight into the president's office, where she told him with quiet dignity —

"I was not hired to be a spy! I do not intend to do the work of a spy!"

He apologized, and personally escorted her to the elevator.

As a good Victorian mother, she had set about making certain her daughters were schooled in the household arts. I have written "daughters"; this was early in the twentieth century; our brother was not taught to cook and clean!

Father liked to cook — certain specialties — and in his own way. He fixed our Sunday night suppers, the roast-vegetables-and-dessert dinner having been prepared at noon by Mother. He frequently made an excellent Welsh rarebit. But once he had the idea he wanted to do popovers.

That first Sunday night they were flat as pancakes. Every succeeding Sunday night he made them and, loyally, we ate them, each weekly batch rising somewhat higher than the one before. The Sunday they popped gloriously all over the iron muffin pans, we cheered and hugged him and ate the hot, crispy-moist, buttery things until we were stuffed.

But only that once! He never made popovers again!

After helping in the kitchen when we were small, learning to beat eggs, roll out cookies, Betty and I took turns one evening a week, cooking and serving the entire dinner. Once a week, our parents patiently ate burned meat, soggy vegetables, runny desserts, until — eventually — we could each put a respectable meal on the table. About then — we were off to college.

Mother made all our dresses when we were small, good quality ready-mades not then being available. And, of course, she taught Betty and me to sew. We did not take to embroidery, but we did come to see the advantages of learning to make clothes for ourselves.

Betty must have been about eleven or twelve years old, when she decided to make herself a party dress. Not that any parties were in the offing, but I think she felt invitations might somehow appear, if she had a dress ready.

Mother had a new sewing machine attachment, which produced a picoted edge. Betty carefully cut yards and yards of lavender organdy ruffles, picoted the edges, ruffled the endless lengths, and then sewed them round and round the skirt, neck, and short, puffed sleeves. Then she tried on the dress.

She stood in front of Mother's long mirror, her dark, curly hair damp on her head, her slight boyish figure encircled from neck to knee with stiff, lavender ruffles — a blueish lavender, that turned her tanned arms and legs a dirty brown.

I know now — young as I was, I knew it then — that she had been expecting the dress would transform a tomboy into a pretty, picture-book party girl.

For long minutes she stood and looked at the stiff, lavender organdy, the thin, brown arms and legs, the sweat-damp hair. Then, without a word, she stepped out of the dress, picked up the shears and cut it to ribbons.

We grew up knowing our parents loved to give us gifts or treats, but that they had financial limits, and we couldn't have everything. As the oldest, I was aware that they were hard put to keep us three in private schools. They believed it was in our best interests; I could not question it. But I could — and did — forego my class ring, because it cost too much.

I had learned — even younger — the lesson of boom and bust.

We were playing hopscotch that spring on the sidewalk, and I had a dime in my pocket. It was what I was paid weekly for darning Father's socks, a task that took at least an hour of concentrated effort. The hole must not be pulled together — that would produce a painful ridge. The thread must be woven in and out, back and forth, to cover the hole and strengthen the surrounding fabric. It was neither easy nor interesting.

As we played that morning, an old man came by selling balloons — wild, beautiful, joyous things, tugging at the strings in his hand. I wanted the blue one, I wanted it more than anything in the world! I fingered the dime in my pocket, pulled it out and handed it over. Took the live, quivering string, with the glorious blue globe dancing at the end.

The string slipped through my fingers, and the balloon sailed off over the treetops.

Years later, I told Mother about this.

"Why didn't you *tell* me?" she sorrowed. "I'd have found you another dime!"

But I was the oldest, the one to "set an example."

"Don't cry over your mistakes! Just don't do it again!" But I did.

It was the Florida real estate speculation craze of the twenties. I "invested" a hard-earned hundred dollars in a scheme promoted by some acquaintances. A hundred dollars was a month's earnings.

C.B. never threw it up to me. Our backgrounds were different. Our values were the same. We both knew money was not the most important thing in the world — not worth inflicting grief or heartache. Living was more important than earning a living.

It is now more than two generations since the five-day workweek was standardized. Without that happening, we could scarcely have planned the move, in the forties, to *The Willows*. Even so, we never subscribed to the concept that five days of work is endurable only because it is followed by a weekend of partying, the attitude expressed by CBS "weatherman," Mark McKewen, bleating fatuously — "Ah — TGIF!"

We had bond salesmen friends, making good money, buying nice homes. But — like my father — C.B. always enjoyed his work. His salary, over the years, never went over $15,000 a year. But, over the years, we managed to own and enjoy four homes.

The American Dream — a home of one's own!

Early in our marriage (we were living in a two-room efficiency in Brooklyn) we went to Long Island with friends who were looking into a new housing development. There I saw what I thought was the home of my dreams: brand new — three bedrooms — a *real* kitchen, not a stove and sink behind a folding door — and a *fireplace!*

The price was $10,500. Could we ever manage such a sum? And if it were as impossible as it seemed, did that mean we could never — ever — own our own home?

Like most Americans, that was what we wanted. The houses we came eventually to buy were all old, empty, in need of repairs. Nobody else had seen their possibilities, so we were able to buy cheaply. Then we used our free time, our extra energy, and our creative abilities to turn these derelicts into desirable homes. We thought it fun!

We also learned it was scary, challenging, difficult — and much more exciting than the movies, or sports, or bridge.

The Wall Street crash of November 1929 did not immediately touch us. Actually, as stock prices continued to fall, we ventured into the market with a couple of hundred dollars, and bought some aircraft stock. C.B. believed aviation had a future.

But in February 1933 *The New York World* was sold. Overnight, it ceased publication, in spite of heroic efforts of the staff. Copyboys, pressmen, reporters and editors were all jobless in the middle of the Great Depression.

There was no unemployment insurance in those days.

An elderly photographer had just arranged to take his sick wife to the hospital.

"How can I tell her I can't do it? How can I tell her I have no money — no job?" he cried — dazed and stricken — to C.B.

"I gave him fifty dollars," C.B. told me later. "I hope it's all right with you."

Our then apartment house backed up on a Brooklyn subway station, where the tracks rose to the surface. After going to bed that night, trying to hide our worries from each other, we were awakened at daybreak by shouting and screaming from the platform below. People were pointing up above our heads! We craned our necks. The apartments above were on fire!

We swept armloads of clothing from the closet. I gathered up my wedding silver, and we followed other night-clad tenants down four flights of stairs.

The fire was quickly extinguished; our apartment was not damaged. And C.B. was one of the lucky ones — he was picked up, almost immediately by the *New York World-Telegram*.

But the Depression deepened. We drove our Model A Ford to an airplane hangar in Connecticut and left it there, since we could neither afford to drive it nor store it. Months later, when we were able to reclaim it, some of C.B.'s many friends in the industry had had it repainted and had put on four new tires!

But long before that, I went one day to buy a pair of shoes. I wrote a check and gave it to the clerk. He handed it back.

"It's no good," he said. I was stunned.

"But of course it is! We've had an account there for a couple of years, and we're *never* overdrawn!"

"The bank closed this morning. All the banks are closed. Hadn't you heard?"

But I hadn't. We didn't own a radio, and I hadn't spent money on a morning paper, because C.B. would later bring home the afternoon *World-Telegram*.

The stock market crash had seemed to concern only the wealthy. The closed banks hit everybody.

President Franklin Roosevelt's famous words today are history: *"The only thing we have to fear is Fear itself."*

It is difficult — in the 1990s — to understand the reassurance these words carried, as they were spoken for the first time, in a strong, warm, confident voice — when the world as we knew it, the country whose strength we had taken for granted — seemed collapsing around us.

The banks opened again. Congress enacted legislation that offered new solutions for old problems. New Deal agencies proliferated. There was a new air of possibility and hope.

Working, then, on an afternoon paper meant daytime hours for C.B. We had a little money saved. Maybe now was the time to look for that home of our own.

We found it in the New Jersey suburbs — six rooms, no central heat, an unkempt lot. The price was $6,000. We took on a $5,000 mortgage, wondering if we would live long enough to pay it off. It was the first time in our lives we had gone into debt for anything.

The last house we bought was C.B.'s grandfather's home in Moorefield; a dilapidated, disintegrating Greek revival brick structure, which Judge Allen — who fathered ten children — hoped would be an ancestral home for generations to come — a hope as doomed as the cause he espoused with all his heart and soul and fortune, the sacred Cause of the Confederacy.

Chapter 14

"A Time To Keep and A Time To Cast Away"

The poor young law student from Woodstock, Virginia, was summoned as a juror in the U.S. District Court in distant Clarksburg, in the 1830s. Passing through Moorefield on the long horseback ride, he — like others before and after him — fell in love with the South Branch Valley of the Potomac, and determined to make it his future home.

J.W.F. Allen was then without friends, money or influence. Moreover, he was a supporter of Andrew Jackson in a county which was nine-tenths Whig backers of Henry Clay.

But — "He opened his office and so conducted himself under these trying circumstances" — says his 1875 obituary in the Romney, West Virginia, *South Branch Intelligencer* — "that he soon had friends and business."

Respect and influence evidently followed, for those Virginia Whigs elected him Judge of the Circuit Court; and judge again, in 1872, in the new state of West Virginia, after he had survived the war and the difficult days of Reconstruction, bankrupt with his Confederate bonds, disbarred and disenfranchised.

When his home, *Ingleside*, came on the market in the 1960s, having passed through several hands (none of which had done much for it), C.B. wanted to try to save it, believing we could restore and then sell it to someone who could appreciate and take proper care of the lovely old place.

Over the unkempt years, it had acquired a reputation for being haunted, as empty houses often do. Folks said the paint wouldn't stay on the south corner, because the original owner had cut his throat in the attic, and the blood had run all the way down the outside!

The fact that there was no attic didn't deter the gossipers. But — ripping away the plaster from the inside — our contractor found that a hundred years of rainwater from blocked gutters, seeping down between the plaster and the old, handmade bricks, had so softened these, that they were about to crumble away.

Legends die hard. Months later, when we were about to open the house for Hardy County's *Heritage Weekend*, three little boys rang the doorbell and asked to be shown "the house with the "h'ants." I said I was sorry, but there were no "h'ants."

"What!" protested a wide-eyed curly-head, "no chains rattling? No blood on the stairs? No skelittings in the cellar?"

"Positively no skelittings!" I said firmly, and offered cookies and a look at C.B.'s airplane pictures to make up for this deficiency.

Ingleside, the Judge J.W.F. Allen home, after the C.B. Allens had rebuilt it.

We had never expected to leave *The Willows*. But the Greek revival house, with the winding walnut staircase, was in such bad shape, it took over a year to complete the restoration. While it was going on, we were beginning to realize that it was now *our* generation that was slowing down, being retired, considering alternative life-styles. Separately, reluctantly, we had reached the same conclusion — but each was afraid to tell the other — that it was time to let go the farm and settle for less acreage, less responsibility.

I used to feel it was pretty rough punishment for the Biblical Lot's Wife to be turned into a pillar of salt, just because she couldn't resist a backward look at the home she had loved and was leaving forever. But, over the years, I have noticed that people seem to lose their joy and juice, when they insist on hanging on to outworn ways and outgrown concepts. Junk accumulates in the mind as well as the attic, and golden hours of living are lost, dragging out old prejudices and pawing through useless possessions.

So we sold *The Willows* and moved into *Ingleside*.

C.B.'s dad was born in that house, and he used to tell how the Yankees sent a troop of cavalry to capture him when he was only three days old!

Union troops were quartered in Moorefield in May of 1863, and some practical joker saw to it that word reached their commander that Lee, Johnson, Jackson and Ashby were all in secret conference up at Judge Allen's place.

Eager to cover himself with glory, and perhaps even end the long conflict, the Yankee captain rounded up his men and surrounded the square, brick plantation house on the low hillside just south of town.

But there were no hoofprints in the dust, no other signs of visitors. All was quiet without, and within was the squall of a very young baby.

"I ask your pardon, ma'am, for intruding at a time like this," the Yankee captain apologized, cap in hand, to the woman in the big walnut bed in the downstairs bedroom.

"But I have information which makes it necessary to search this place."

"I can't stop you," she told him, "but you'll find no one here but the children and the servants."

Sometime later he had to admit that she was right.

"I may as well tell you," he said before leaving, "we had positive information that Lee, Jackson, Johnson and Ashby were all here."

She may have smiled a little at that.

"Your informer was correct. Here" (and she motioned toward the young son, who stood silent and abashed by the bedside) "is Leigh. The little colored boy over there is Jackson, and his mother, my nurse, is Charity Ann Johnson.

"And here" (turning back the bed covers) "is Ashby! William
Turner Ashby Allen, born three days ago!"

Carrie Williams Allen must have been a confident and capable
woman. Two years before, she had written a brother — "When we
hear they are coming, we get the most valuable things out of the
way. The last time . . . I hid all the liquor, silver, guns and ammuni-
tion and my sewing machine. And then I sat down very quietly
to await their arrival, and was somewhat disappointed that they
did not come. We have sent Mr. Allen's library to a place of
safety . . . They always inquire particularly for Mr. Allen. I suppose
you have heard they put a price on his head, $1,500. He has been
traveling about a good deal . . . I beg him not to come home until
we have force enough to protect him."

In an old man's memories, eighty years later, it was "Black
Mammy," standing silent but strongly protective, as long as the
Yankee officer was in that room, who emerged as the central figure
in Willie Allen's childhood.

With every family need in short supply or impossible to come
by, Carrie Allen, nevertheless, did her capable best to bear and raise
her children and look after the house and farm. When the war
ended, the Judge was forbidden to practice law. The only way he
could earn a living for himself and his family was to go into practice
with a young lawyer who could take the required loyalty oath. Joe
Sprig had not fought against the Union; he had hired a substitute.

"Black Mammy" took Willie berrying in the woods; she let him
help her make persimmon beer, and go down into the damp cellar
to feed cornmeal to the live oysters in the barrel the Judge had had
sent from Baltimore. She told him to pick up a girl's handkerchief
and return it with a bow, when he went to his first dance at the
age of seven. And she frequently warned him that, if he didn't mend
his ways, a "ha'nt" would surely get him! If more drastic correction
was necessary, she administered it.

"Black Mammy," — the little boy sniffed at the kitchen door like
a hound-puppy — "what smells so good cookin!?"

"I'se fryin' chicken fo' d'ladies come he'p yo' Mammy wid dey
all-day quiltin'," she told him. "You bring Black Mammy in some
stove wood an' she fix you a plate."

"I had every intention of gettin' that wood," Dad would explain.
"But when I went outside, a big yellow butterfly come along an'
I went after it. Pretty soon, Black Mammy, she hollered —

'You Willie! Whe's m' stove wood?'

"Then I hollered back — 'Yah! Yah! I don't hafta get wood for you, you black nigger, you!' and I went off after the butterfly.

"But after a while, I was so hungry, I come back and begged — 'Black Mammy, couldn't you gimme jesta little bitta chicken?' "

" 'You come ri'chere, Willie,' she said, 'an Ah'll fix you.'

"An' then she grab me and tucked my head between her knees an' whaled me good!

" 'Jedge tell me neveh let one'a yo' chillern call me old black niggah!' "

Chasing yellow butterflies ended at thirteen, when the Judge died, and Dad went to work to help educate his younger brothers and sisters. His first job was shucking corn from daylight to dark, for which he was paid a paper quarter and told to board himself. Years later, when he shared our New Jersey home, he thought it incredible that I would pay fifty cents a dozen for eggs!

Each generation is appalled at the profligacy of its children and grandchildren. My generation certainly did not expect the American dream (a home of one's own) to be realized immediately after marriage, and to come with a two-car garage and custom draperies.

I wonder today, if that may not be reversed, and if our children's children, paying off our billions of national and consumer debt, may not marvel at the extravagances of their parents and grandparents.

We live twice as long today, but we are obsessed with the pressure of time. In 1900, life expectancy was only 26 years compared with today's 75. President Jefferson carried out scientific experiments in his gardens. President Coolidge is said to have napped a lot. President Bush bangs about in a high-powered boat... Does fast transportation dispose us to think we can deal with problems as easily as we do distances?

Time... I was eleven years old, when I was awakened one night by my parents and taken to their bedroom window to see the wonder of Halley's Comet. On that particular passage within sight of earth — unlike its recent one in 1985-86 — it was a great glowing star, with a tail spilling over half the sky.

But I grumbled and fussed because I had been waked from a sound sleep, refused to marvel at the sight, and demanded to be put back to bed.

Perhaps, in 1986, I was subconsciously trying to atone for such behavior, when I helped a great-nephew, an award-winning young science teacher in the coal mine area of West Virginia, to take a trip to Australia to photograph the comet on its most recent — and disappointing — appearance.

Time... Many years ago, a German pioneer named Dahle became the owner of acres and acres of high mountain land south of Moorefield. In the slang of that day, it was referred to as "Dahle's sods." It is now Dolly Sods, a National Wilderness area, beloved by some of us who visit it frequently, because of its extraordinary diversity and scenic splendor. Up there, one begins to *feel* and *see* Time...

Dolly Sods in summer, with rocks and one-sided spruce.

Although the glaciers did not quite reach West Virginia, the resulting cold climate helped produce the "rock streams"; and the great winds, howling along the Allegheny Front, sculpted them, leaving the fantastic jumble of white rocks one marvels at today.

Small arctic plants grow there in the crevices, as well as the more familiar, temperate zone shrubs. Red spruce branches extend outward only on one side of these massed evergreens, because of the strong winds that still sweep the Front — this boundary between the ridge-and-valley country to the east, and the Allegheny Plateau to the west.

You are looking at geological time in the jumble of great rocks, at recent years of evergreen growth in the one-sided trees, and at one season's spurt of wild azaleas and huckleberries. And you, yourself, can ingest it all in a couple of hours, along with your sandwich and coffee!

I drive back down the mountainside, and back along the busy highway, rested — refreshed; not so concerned with the evening news, and with no interest at all in "Entertainment Tonight."

Time... "The time to take doughnuts" C.B.'s dad used to say — "is when doughnuts is passed!"

I try to remember that when my urban American reaction to a suggestion that we head for the hills for a day, is to say — "Oh, I wish I could! But I don't have the *time*."

The four lane highways are not the only way to travel. They may be the quickest way to reach a particular destination in a given length of time. But the trip itself is what you should want to remember; that is, if you really have looked at and enjoyed the scenery, talked with the people you've met along the way, and not complained too much about the food and the accommodations.

C.B. and I missed *our* fiftieth anniverary by three years. Our last party was December 31, 1970 at *Ingleside*. I remember we always had good parties, with firelight and friends, good talk, good food — and not too much to drink.

It started snowing early that afternoon, and it kept up, ever more thickly. By five o'clock it was too deep for traveling, but by then it was also too late to postpone the party. We lit fires in all the fireplaces, and turned on every light in the house, so that anyone brave enough to venture out, could plainly see that guests were welcome at *Ingleside*.

And everybody came! Walking, mostly, and piling snowy boots and coats on newspapers in the hall. And the party was all the more fun for the dishevelment within, and the deepening drifts without.

After we had welcomed the year 1971, C.B. tried to drive a few guests back downtown. But his car stuck in the drifts on the way back, and he had to abandon it, and trudge the final stretch back uphill.

I waited by the window, watching — in the first hours of the new year — as he slogged slowly back up the hill. His head was bent. Was it the storm, or did he seem more tired than usual? There had been forty-seven years of waiting for him to come home — from work and from the world's far places. But I don't think I ever resented being the one to wait at home. At any given moment, one gives, the other takes. Sometimes it evens out, sometimes it seems not to. In the end, it is what you feel you are getting. I always felt I was getting a very full and interesting life — even if it didn't always work out the way I planned.

The first year of our marriage had been a strenuous one, as C.B. worked nights and I, daytimes, and our two-room Greenwich Village apartment was up five steep flights of stairs.

Edna St. Vincent Millay once wrote:

> *My candle burns at both ends*
> *It will not last the night.*
> *But Ah! my foes and Oh! my friends*
> *It gives a lovely light!*

She was a senior the year I entered Vassar, so I only knew her from afar. Just before her class's graduation, gossip swept the dormitories that she had stayed off-campus the previous evening until nearly midnight, and thus might not be allowed to receive her diploma!

What changes women's colleges have seen in 75 years!

But for young people then or now, regular meals and enough sleep are the last things to worry about. I went to a doctor one day, because I was tired all the time, underweight and coughing a lot.

In 1925 nobody would have blamed that on smoking. Billboard tobacco ads were showing a pretty girl saying to the young man beside her, who had just lit a cigarette — "Blow some my way!" Smoking was smart. But C.B. didn't — until he returned from World War II — and I'd found I didn't really enjoy it.

The doctor found a small spot on one lung, and said the then-dreaded word — *tuberculosis*.

That was like hearing today the word *cancer*. There were no antibiotics in the early twenties; tuberculosis could be a death sentence. "Curing" was the prescription. "Curing" was bedrest — in a sanitorium — eating nourishing meals and getting lots of sleep.

I sat, that afternoon, on the steps of the New York Public Library, near its majestic lions, thinking — "Is this all there is? Is my life over at 25? Why am I being given so little *time?*"

When I returned from a TB sanitorium in North Carolina six months later, I was beginning to learn that sometimes one hangs on by letting go.

C.B. and I were both past seventy, when we happily ushered in the year of 1971. I have survived him now for over twenty years.

Time... I want to say to today's eager young women — Don't hurry so! You have no idea how much time you have! You can have it all (or almost all) but not necessarily all at once. Most of us will no longer spend our lives in one place or work at only one kind of job. We shall probably live in a dozen different places and do all sorts of different things, including raising a family.

So — there is plenty of time — if we will take it — for the children.

Time... The robins raised two broods this spring in a well-built nest on the downspout under my eaves. In an uncertain world, it is good to know there are still young robins. I don't hear them often now — it is their moulting time. In another month they will be gathering in loose groups, running about, suddenly lifting off together. And then — one early fall day — I shall suddenly realize they have all gone.

They carry no road maps either, but they will be on course, and making — I hope — a safe journey toward the unknown.

I anticipate the same for myself.